THE NEW ENGLISH BIBLE REVIEWED

THE NEW ENGLISH BIBLE REVIEWED

edited by

DENNIS NINEHAM

LONDON
EPWORTH PRESS

FIRST PUBLISHED IN 1965

© EPWORTH PRESS 1965

Book Steward
FRANK H. CUMBERS

SET IN MONOTYPE PLANTIN AND PRINTED IN
GREAT BRITAIN BY THE CAMELOT PRESS LTD
LONDON AND SOUTHAMPTON

CONTENTS

ACKNOWLEDGMENTS

The *New English Bible*, copyright 1961, 1970 by the Oxford University Press, 1970. We acknowledge with gratitude permission to reproduce quotations in this volume, and also wish to acknowledge to the authors most without exception in the editor and publishers of the journals and books, from which the following references are taken. Detailed references are indicated at beginning of each chapter.

ACKNOWLEDGEMENTS

The *New English Bible* is copyright Oxford and Cambridge University Presses 1961. We acknowledge with gratitude permission to reproduce extracts from it in this volume, and also express our sincere thanks for their most willing co-operation to the editors and publishers of the journals and books from which the following reviews are taken. Detailed references are supplied at the beginning of each chapter.

GLOSSARY

AV   *The Authorized Version* published in 1611, based largely on William Tyndale's translation.

KJV   *King James Version.* The American way of referring to the above.

RV   *The Revised Version.* A revision of the above by a group of English scholars of various denominations, working in close co-operation with a similar group of American scholars. Published between 1881 and 1885.

ASV   *American Standard Version.* The version of the above published in America in 1901 which embodied a small number of different renderings preferred by the American scholars associated in the joint work.

RSV   *Revised Standard Version.* A revision of the above by a group of distinguished American scholars, of which the New Testament was published first in 1946 and then, in a somewhat amended form, together with the Old Testament, in 1952. Apocrypha published 1957.

Introduction

D. E. NINEHAM

IT IS an open secret that, so far as sales are concerned, the *NEB* New Testament has been a success beyond even the most sanguine expectation; in the course of four years well over 6,000,000 copies have been sold. No one of course knows how many of those copies have been read; but the initial reaction of those who did read their copies and expressed an opinion was, on balance, distinctly favourable. As time has gone on, however, some have thought they could detect a growing disenchantment with the *NEB*. Are they right, and, if so, what are the reasons for this disenchantment?

It is well that these questions should be raised at the present time. Before many years are out the Old Testament and Apocrypha will be published in the new version and then a number of people will have to make decisions about the use of the *NEB*. In the last resort, the only test of any translation is the extent to which it commends itself in use; no translation, however, can commend itself in this way unless it is given a chance to do so. In what ways should the *NEB* be tried out? What uses is it good for? What purposes can it, and was it meant to, serve? Designed primarily for private reading, it has already been quite widely used in public worship, though mainly for reading by a single voice and not for congregational recitation or chanting. Is this the right pattern for the future? The possible use of the *NEB* in education raises further questions. For example, its use in schools to stimulate fresh interest and give children a new feeling for the contemporary relevance of the Bible is quite a different matter from its use in examination papers, or as the basis of biblical commentaries, where a closer and more literal translation might well be thought to have advantages.

This volume of reviews has been prepared in the hope that it may stimulate discussion of such questions and perhaps help towards the responsible answering of them.

Limitation of space has meant a high degree of selectivity. A considerable number of reviews have been read which are not represented here at all; and even of those which do appear, few have been able to be printed in full. However, great care has been taken to make the selection as genuinely representative as possible. In the nature of the case, the reviews overlapped a good deal, particularly in what they had to say about the historical origins of the *NEB* and the way the translators' work was organized. Consequently, it was possible to make quite extensive cuts in the reviews selected for reproduction without too serious loss. To ensure that these cuts involved no significant distortion, every review was submitted, in precisely the form here printed, to its original author, who in each case very kindly—though often naturally with some reluctance—sanctioned the cuts; the reader can thus be assured that though the cuts are in some cases very considerable, they do not involve any misrepresentation of the reviewer's basic judgement.

Likewise, in selecting the reviews to be represented, every effort has been made to provide a fair cross-section of those which have come to the editor's notice. In one respect this is particularly important. It will be noticed that of the reviews represented here, those written by New Testament specialists are on the whole favourable, while those written by literary critics are markedly less so. The same distinction was observable in the notices which it has not been possible to reproduce. On the basis of all the reviews examined it is a fair generalization to say that reviewers whose chief criterion was fidelity to the original Greek have fairly consistently given this translation better marks than those who judged primarily by aesthetic criteria.

Another point worth making is that the small number of reviews reproduced here which attack the new version on grounds of doctrinal bias or error is a fair indication of how few reviews of this kind have appeared, at any rate in periodicals known to the editor. It should perhaps be added that those which have come to light have in almost every case appeared in the organs of groups rather on the fringes of the main stream of Church life.

The high proportion of American and Canadian reviews among those selected for inclusion is deliberate. Far more full-scale reviews appeared on the other side of the Atlantic than in this country, and many of them were in periodicals not easily accessible over here, so that English readers would not have been likely to see what they said apart from some such volume as this.

In the main it is hoped that this collection will speak for itself, but two or three comments may perhaps be in order.

On the question of the origin of the new translation and the way it was produced, little needs to be added to the very clear statement by Bishop Williams in the preface he contributed to it. It is true that in a letter to the *Times Literary Supplement* (No. 3,289, March 11th, 1965, p. 195), Professor G. R. Driver traces the origin of the new version back to a proposal for a revision of the Revised Version made by the University presses before the war and states categorically that 'no church had any hand in the inception of the project'. In fact, however, the connexion between the *NEB* and these earlier proposals was a good deal more tenuous than Professor Driver's words might suggest, and the churches—particularly the Church of Scotland, and the Presbytery of Stirling and Dunblane, from whom the proposal originated first of all—should not be deprived of the credit for taking what was in effect a quite new initiative.

Readers may also like to know a little more than the preface tells them about how the translators worked. The seven members of the translators' panel divided the various books of the New Testament between them and each one produced a draft translation of the books assigned to him. These drafts were then circulated to all the members, who worked on them at a series of residential conferences until a version had been arrived at on which all could agree. In this form it was passed on to the literary panel whose members, without necessarily claiming any expert knowledge of the original language, were equipped to judge the translators' work from the point of view of its English style. They could say, in effect: 'this may be what the Greek means, but it is not good current English; we suggest such and such amendments.' To which the panel of translators was free to reply: 'The amended version may be good English but it is not what the Greek means' —and so the dialogue between the two panels would go on until a version was reached which satisfied the members of both. At this stage a book was ready for the comments of the Joint Committee and if passed by them, was filed to await the process of final revision when all the books had passed both panels and could be reviewed together. Whatever may be thought of this procedure, it will be obvious that few things are likely to have crept into the *NEB* by inadvertence!

So far as the resulting literary style is concerned, it is no part of the editor's task to defend the translators and the members of the literary panel, even were he competent to do so; and it would be presumptuous of him to try. In fact he has some sympathy with some of the criticisms that have been made. In places it is hard to resist the conclusion that the translators were seduced by the delusive ideal of a timeless English style into using expressions which are not genuinely current usage with any contemporary group. Nevertheless, there is real point in the following words of a recent writer in the *Times Literary Supplement*:[1]

'Both inside and outside the churches the view is expressed that passing from the AV to the *NEB* marks a decline in purely literary quality in some parts of the New Testament, but the comparison of literary quality is often made on the basis of few passages, and with little regard for the uneven literary quality of the original Greek which, largely masked in the King James version, emerges more sharply in the new translation. When the new translation of the Old Testament comes to be published the many differences of style between the original books may be even more evident; the Old Testament books were, after all, the work of many more and diverse hands than was the case with the New Testament and their authorship spread over a longer period.'

That is surely well said; and it is a perfectly possible criticism of the Authorized Version that it muffles the wide variety of Greek styles to be found in the New Testament—some of them far from fluent—under the single blanket of a sonorous, but undifferentiated, English prose.[2]

Thirdly, it may be worth spelling out for the general reader a point presupposed in many of the scholarly reviews. Anyone who has attempted to copy out documents of any length knows that some mistakes inevitably creep in, however much care is taken to

---

[1] 17th March 1965, quoted by kind permission.

[2] Since individual passages of the AV are so often praised as striking and memorable in contrast to their counterparts in the *NEB*, it may perhaps be permissible to point out that there are also passages where the advantage seems to be on the other side. Cf., for example, the striking phrases in 2 Cor. 6[8, 10], 'we are the impostors who speak the truth, the unknown men whom all men know . . . penniless we own the world'. And every reader should compare the two versions at 2 Cor 6[11–13] where a passage so badly translated in the AV as to be virtually meaningless, fully regains its moving appeal in the fine rendering of the *NEB*.

avoid them. So when we remember the innumerable times the
New Testament books were copied during the 1300 years or so
before the invention of printing, it will not be surprising that, of
the thousands of hand-written copies which have survived, no
two are exactly alike. But, surprising or not, the fact presents the
translator with a problem. In any given passage, which version is
he to translate as being most likely to reproduce what the New
Testament writer originally wrote ?[3] The science of textual criticism exists to help in answering such questions, and in the last
100 years or so—not to say the last 350 years—New Testament
textual criticism has made great strides. For one thing, many
handwritten copies have come to light which were previously
unknown and are in many cases older than those known before;
and also methods for deciding which copy is likely to give the true
reading have been elaborated and refined. The translators of the
NEB New Testament are very modest about their competence and
achievements in this field (see, for example, the introduction to
the Library Edition, pp. vii and viii), but the publication of the
Greek text on which they worked[4] shows how much thought
they gave to this matter; and the reader can be assured that whatever he may think of their actual translation, the Greek text it
represents is pretty certainly far closer to what was originally
written than the text underlying any previous English translation.[5]
In this respect the *NEB* is a very considerable advance on the
AV. In order to judge the sort of difference involved the reader
may consult such passages as Mt 6[13], Lk 22[19b & 20], Jn 8[1-11],
1 Jn 5[7-8], or Mk 16[9ff], though in the last case, it must be admitted,
the *NEB* hardly makes clear that no competent scholar regards
16[9-20] as part of what Mark wrote.

Since many of the reviewers discuss the fact that the Greek text
on which the *NEB* is based is an "eclectic" text, it may be well to
say something about the meaning of this technical term. As
every manuscript is copied, or "descended", from one or more
earlier ones, it is possible to trace the genealogical trees of manuscripts and to classify them in "families" which often derive from
a single area and seem to have been subject to the same sort of
influences. Consequently, they display similar characteristics,

[3] The autograph, i.e. the original as penned by the New Testament author
himself, has in every case perished.
[4] *The Greek New Testament*, ed. R. V. G. Tasker, O.U.P. and C.U.P., 1964.
[5] This judgement implies no comment on the *American RSV*.

e.g. a tendency to expand or abbreviate a certain type of passage in a similar sort of way. Some textual critics have made a great deal of this in their efforts to recover the original text; they argue that the known characteristics of some families make their evidence suspect, at any rate in certain types of passage, and so they prefer to follow the reading of what they regard as the "best" families of manuscripts, unless in any particular case there are special reasons for doing otherwise. Most of the printed editions of the Greek New Testament are based on a consistent preference for certain types, or families, of manuscripts. By contrast, an eclectic procedure is one in which each passage which gives rise to a textual problem is treated on its own merits and the readings of the various manuscripts at that point are weighed, without prejudice, in the light of the considerations which apply to that particular passage. The matter is one of emphasis; no scholar advocates either procedure to the complete exclusion of the other, but a text based mainly on the second procedure is known as an "eclectic" text. The translators of the *NEB* New Testament did not translate any of the existing printed Greek texts, but produced an "eclectic" text of their own, through discussion of each textually difficult passage as they came to translate it. In the book referred to above, Dr. Tasker, one of the translators, has incorporated the results of these discussions into a complete Greek text of the New Testament and added a brief account of the reasons which led to the final decision in each case.

Finally, something must be said about charges of doctrinal error. Those who make such charges against the *NEB* are comparatively few, as we have seen; none the less, it is important that they should be clear what they are doing. So far as Christians are committed to the text of the Bible as their final authority in matters of faith and morals, their commitment is presumably to the original text, as far as textual criticism can recover it, and to whichever interpretation the best modern study may suggest. If in the light of sober scholarship we should be driven to the conclusion that the true text or the true meaning were different from what used to be supposed, then it would surely be for us to make any doctrinal adjustments that might be necessitated. In fact it is doubtful if anything of this sort arises in connexion with this new version, but the principle needs to be affirmed. To condemn any version for failure to support certain doctrinal positions is to put the cart before the horse. It is to set up the views of some post-New Testament Christians, whether the Reformers or the translators of the AV or whoever it may be, as judges of what the word of God *must* have said or *must* have meant. Some such procedure may be justified in the case of those who hold—as the Roman Catholic Church perhaps does—that alongside the authority of the Bible there is some other authority competent to lay down which version is the true vehicle of revelation and to decide by means other than scholarly study what that version really means. But those who have brought doctrinal charges against the *NEB* have not for the most part given any sign of holding such a view. So their charges can only be justified if the translators of the *NEB* were motivated, consciously or unconsciously, by consistent doctrinal bias. So far as conscious bias goes the editor knows enough of the translators and of the way they worked to be able to say categorically that the charge is false; unconscious bias is much harder to disprove, but readers will observe that none of the writers represented in this volume with an established scholarly reputation has seen much trace of such bias, and they can be assured that the same is true of all the other scholars whose reviews came to notice but could not be reproduced.

It remains only to thank Mrs Emily Boone for her work in typing and correcting proofs and the Reverend Michael Perry of the S.P.C.K. for undertaking a great deal of editorial work without which this book could never have been got ready for press.

New Testament Studies[1]

FRANK W. BEARE

... IT HAS the great merit of reading, not like a translation from a foreign language, but like a work of contemporary English prose. The style is clear, vigorous, and simple; the vocabulary is seldom colloquial, never stilted, but consistently drawn from that in common use. At times, the reader feels a certain lack of richness, of elevation, of the poetic spark that can set hearts aflame; to compensate for that, he is seldom left in doubt about the meaning of what he is reading. There is an unusually high percentage of monosyllables, and long unwieldy periods are broken up into short sentences (for instance, Ephesians 1³⁻¹⁴, a single sentence in Greek, appears in two paragraphs and eight sentences in the new English rendering). 'We have conceived our task', the translators tell us, 'to be that of understanding the original as precisely as we could (using all available aids), and then saying again in our own native idiom what we believed the author to be saying in his.' They were 'enjoined to replace Greek constructions and idioms by those of contemporary English', and they have carried out the injunction faithfully.

The form and arrangement are also modern.... The old chapter and verse divisions are ... replaced, substantially, by a limited number of larger divisions, with subject-headings. In the Gospel according to Matthew, for instance, there are eight main divisions, to which the following headings have been given: 'The Coming of Christ'; 'The Sermon on the Mount'; 'Teaching and Healing'; 'Controversy'; 'Jesus and His Disciples'; 'Challenge to Jerusalem'; 'Prophecies and Warnings'; 'The Final Conflict'. Any system of divisions might be open to question; but it seems fair to express surprise that the editors have seen fit to disregard the five-fold division of this book, which all critics recognize as the pattern devised by the author himself. Is it really legitimate, when the book has a conscious design, to impose upon it a new pattern of our

[1] Vol. VIII, No. 1 (October, 1961), pp. 80–92.

creation? In Mark and Luke, the first of these headings and the last two appear again, except that in Luke, 'the Messiah' replaces 'Christ'; if there is a reason for this alteration, it is not apparent. The second division bears the same title in Mark and Luke—namely, 'In Galilee: Success and Opposition'; but in Luke this division includes the parallels to Mark 5^{1}-9^{41}, which in Mark fall into the third division ('Miracles of Christ'), and in part even into the fourth ('Growing Tension'). The central section of Luke (often called his 'Travel-Narrative') is here given the heading, 'Journeys and Encounters'. The various committees no doubt considered the form of these headings, and settled upon them after full debate; but I would still venture to question the wisdom of using identical headings for different masses of materials. The question becomes still more acute when we find that the first chapter of John is given the same heading as the opening of the Synoptics—that is, 'The Coming of Christ'. Thus under this heading we have the genealogy and birth narratives of Matthew, plus the baptism and temptation and the call of the first disciples; in Mark, there is nothing but the baptism and temptation; in Luke, the double annunciation and birth narratives, the visits to Jerusalem, and the baptism, genealogy, and temptation; and in John, we have not one single item from among all these, but read instead the great Prologue, the recognition by John, and the varied testimonies of the first disciples. It seems to me that the fourfold employment of the identical title for such disparate materials is misleading and undesirable. It can hardly be doubted that these objections were raised in committee; it is a pity that they were not allowed to prevail.

The *pericope adulterae* (in TR and AV, John 7^{53}-8^{1}), which in *RSV* is printed in small italics at the foot of the page, is here given a page of its own, following the Gospel of John, under the heading 'An Incident in the Temple', with a brief note about the textual data. This is an excellent way of treating the problem presented by this passage. It is regrettable that the secondary character of the Marcan endings was not made equally clear. It is scarcely too much to say that the handling of the Marcan endings misrepresents the facts and can hardly fail to leave the untutored reader with a totally wrong impression. At the end of verse 8, we are referred to a footnote which reads: 'At this point some of the most ancient witnesses bring the book to a close.' This will hardly make the ordinary reader aware that no serious critic in the world would dream of maintaining that the true text of Mark continues beyond this point in any extant manuscript, and that many good scholars—perhaps a majority—would hold that the book originally ended with the words, 'for they were afraid'. There is no debate about the spuriousness of the supplements found in various manuscripts; the debate is solely over the question whether Mark wrote an ending which has been lost, or whether he intended verse 8 to be his ending. This ought to be clearly reflected in the way in which these spurious endings are printed; instead, the text continues in the same type, and with the conventional verse numbers, separated only by open spaces such as are used in several places to indicate natural breaks in the narrative. The textual notes are inadequate and even vague; they certainly do not suffice to make the situation clear. At the very least, the spurious passages should be bracketed; at best, they should be relegated to footnotes, and printed in small italics, as in *RSV*.

The Greek text which has been used for the translation was established by the translators as they went along. Nothing is said about the principles which guided them in their choice of readings. To me, it is very doubtful that a sound text can be established by a committee which confines itself to the consideration of particular readings as they come. In practice, they must use a modern printed text as their base, and depart from it only when some member of the group raises the question at a given point. It would be utterly impossible for a panel of translators, no matter how competent some of its members might be in the field of textual criticism, to make an independent investigation of all the factors that must be weighed in constituting a text. It would seem much more advisable to follow one of the existing texts consistently (Westcott and Hort, or Nestle), and to depart from it only when the majority of the committee could be convinced that a given reading must be rejected in the light of the latest evidence; any such departures from the printed text could easily be mentioned in footnotes or in an appended list. The reader would then know precisely what Greek reading is rendered in each instance.

This is a large question, and calls for further comment. Goodspeed, though himself a textual scholar of no ordinary stature, contented himself with translating the text as established by Westcott and Hort. The Revisers of 1881 made their selections of readings as they went along; and no one today would look upon their text (reconstituted in Souter's Oxford text) as anything but a half-baked creation, the result of an uneasy compromise between the textual theories of Westcott and Hort and a lingering reverence for the *Textus Receptus*. Since that time much valuable new material has come into our hands—great manuscripts like the Freer codex of the Gospels (W); and above all papyri, some as early as the second and third centuries, now numbering more than seventy, containing fragments of almost all the books of the New Testament and in some cases books in their entirety. Much work has been done on the analysis of the minuscules, especially in the identification of families (Family 1, Family 13, Family 2412, etc.) and in the groupings devised by Von Soden. A beginning has been made in the scientific study of the lectionary text. The evidence of the early versions and of a number of the Fathers has been made available in much greater fullness and accuracy. Hort's theory of a 'Neutral' text, substantially represented by the agreement of B and Aleph, has been generally abandoned; and the translators are entirely justified in the statement that 'there is not at the present time any critical text which would command the same degree of general acceptance as the Revisers' text did in its day' (p. vii). They plead, on the basis of such considerations as these, that they 'could do no other than consider variant readings on their merits, and, having weighed the evidence for themselves, select for translation in each passage the reading which to the best of their judgement seemed most likely to represent what the author wrote. Where other readings seemed to deserve serious consideration they have been recorded in footnotes'; and with the admission that 'their judgement is at best provisional', they express the belief that the text which underlies their version is 'an improvement on that underlying the earlier translations' (pp. vii, viii). This claim may be allowed, provided that an exception be made for the text underlying the *Revised Standard Version*, which was constructed in much the same fashion, with the same range of materials, and by an equally competent group of scholars. In both cases, we are left in some degree of uncertainty about the wording of the Greek text which the translators have chosen; we are given no indication of the principles that have determined their choice of variants; and we cannot be certain that the same principles have been consistently applied throughout the work.

The proof of the pudding is in the eating, and we may now go on to take a few samples. . . .

I propose . . . to examine the textual notes on the first five chapters of Acts in some detail. Ten variants are mentioned in footnotes, against 157 lines of the Nestle apparatus. In *RSV* no variants whatever are noted in these chapters. In *NEB* the notes run as follows:

1²⁶ (Matthias), who was then assigned a place among the twelve apostles. *Footnote:* Some witnesses read 'was then appointed a colleague of the eleven apostles'.
I cannot make out what this note is meant to convey. So far as I can learn, the only significant variant here is the $\iota\beta$ ('twelve') of D, and this appears to have no support except in a passage of Eusebius. There are variants in the prepositional prefix of the verb (singular readings in D and in Aleph), but these would not affect the translation into English. The translation and its accompanying note certainly convey the impression that the variants are much more substantial; and do not indicate the immense weight of support for the reading 'eleven'.

2⁵ devout Jews. *Footnote:* Some witnesses read 'devout men'.
A strange way to put it. The fact is that all witnesses—at least, all that I can conveniently check—read $\check{a}\nu\delta\rho\epsilon\varsigma\ \epsilon\dot{v}\lambda\alpha\beta\epsilon\hat{\iota}\varsigma$ ('devout men'); Aleph omits ' $Iov\delta\alpha\hat{\iota}o\iota$ ('Jews'), but this is a singular reading.

2²⁴ of death. *Footnote:* Some witnesses read 'of Hades'.
The only Greek MS which reads $\H{a}\delta ov$ is D, which often allows its Greek text to be determined by the Latin on the opposite page. The Latin versions consistently read '*inferni*'. Where textual notes are so severely limited, was this one needed?

2³⁷ Peter and the apostles. *Footnote:* Some witnesses read 'the rest of the apostles'.
In fact, D is the only important Greek manuscript which omits $\lambda o\iota\pi o\acute{v}\varsigma$; it is taken into the text by Hort, Nestle, Bover, Soden, and the British and Foreign Bible Society's most recent editors.

3²¹ omit $\dot{a}\pi\ a\dot{\iota}\hat{\omega}vo\varsigma$. *Footnote:* Some witnesses add 'from the beginning of the world'.

Here again D is the only important Greek witness for the omission. It is supported by the Egyptian versions and by some Latin witnesses (OL, Tertullian; Latin translations of Irenaeus and Origen); the Vulgate reads 'a saeculo'.

4¹ chief priests. *Footnote:* Some witnesses omit 'chief'.
In fact the only witnesses for ἀρχιερεῖς are B and C (with Armenian support). Should this be allowed to outweigh the agreement of all the other MSS and versions, except on Hort's over-valuation of B? And what has now become of the reverence for D which has determined the choice of the three preceding variants as noted?

4⁶ Jonathan. *Footnote:* Some witnesses read 'John'.
D ('Ιωναθάς) comes triumphantly back into its own, being allowed to outweigh all the rest of the evidence (apart from OL).

4¹¹. *Footnote:* Some witnesses insert 'and no other'.
In this instance, the evidence for the addition is negligible.

4¹². There is no salvation in anyone else at all. *Footnote:* Some witnesses omit 'There is no . . . at all'.
No evidence for this omission can be cited except for a very few Latin witnesses. D, however, omits ἡ σωτηρία and one is tempted to suspect that this footnote reflects again the exaggerated respect for D that has given rise to several of the others.

4²⁵. by the Holy Spirit. *Footnote:* Some witnesses omit 'by the Holy Spirit'.
The textual tradition here is quite confused. This phrase is omitted by virtually all the Byzantine manuscripts; the omission has all the appearance of an editorial attempt to bring order out of chaos. The evidence of the primary uncials and the versions shows quite unmistakably that πνεύματος ἁγίου belongs in the text; but there is some deep-seated corruption in the text of the verse as a whole.

Without pursuing the examination any farther, there is surely enough here to illustrate the needless difficulties that are incurred in the attempt to establish your text as you go, and to justify the suspicion that no general theory of the text has been consistently applied. If the time has not come to construct a new text which might hope to win general acceptance, as the translators themselves tell us (p. vii), how could it be wise for them to attempt such a task as a *parergon*?—for that is all it could be. My impression is that the final result would not have been greatly different if they had simply translated the Nestle text (not that it is perfect, but simply that it is the most most widely used text of the Greek New Testament in existence)—always permitting themselves a limited discretion to choose a particular variant. Would it even now be an impossible task for them, or some of their number, to draw up and publish a collation, using Nestle or any other good modern text as the base, to enable us to see for ourselves the precise text on which their translation is based?[2]

The work of translation in itself is excellent. It is easy, of course, to find instances of infelicities and to set them against turns of phrase in AV which are far more appealing, and on this basis to disparage the translation as a whole; but this is patently unfair. The new translation will be found readable—and intelligible—by countless people who can make nothing of the archaic language of AV, and have simply given up the effort to read it. Infelicities there are, as there could not fail to be in so large a work of translation, in spite of all the checks devised to eliminate them; and in some of the most familiar passages the new version does not compare in beauty with AV. . . .

But if our attention is drawn to certain infelicities, we ought in fairness to take note of the many passages in which the new translation is infinitely superior to the old, not merely in clarity but also in beauty. But in fact such comparisons ought not to be made. These translators are not revisers, and they have not set themselves to produce a work that would displace the Authorized Version, or to put it forward in any spirit of rivalry. They have sought to produce—and they have succeeded in producing—a work that will 'open the truth of the scriptures to many who have been hindered in their approach to it by barriers of language' (p. xi).

If the Bible is to be valued as the record and medium of divine revelation, and not primarily treasured as splendid literature, it is essential that it should always be given to the people in language that the simplest of them can understand. For this, the Authorized Version no longer serves.

[2] This has now (1964) been done (Ed.). See p. xiii and n. 3.

A Canadian reader, standing with one foot in each world, is frequently made aware of the great and growing differences in English usage on the two sides of the Atlantic. The language of the *New English Bible* is distinctly English (sometimes, I think, peculiarly Scottish) 'English'. In the Sabbath-controversy of Mark 2²³⁻⁴ and parallels, *RSV* uses 'grainfields' and 'ears of grain'; in *NEB* these become 'cornfields' and 'ears of corn'. In the parable of the Leaven (Mt. 13³³, Lk 13²¹), the 'three measures of meal' become in *NEB* 'half a hundredweight of flour'; apart from the greater freedom of this rendering, the phrase 'half a hundred-weight' (while perfectly intelligible) would not be used by an American writer in the context—he would be more likely to put 'three sacks of flour'. (In passing, let me remark that I do not see much point in speaking of 'yeast' at the beginning of this passage, and retaining the verb 'leavened' at the end.) The Tares of the parable (Mt 13²⁴ᶠᶠ·) have become 'weeds' in *RSV* and 'darnel' in *NEB*. I do not know whether 'darnel' is a familiar word in Britain; I can only say that I myself have never encountered it except in commentaries on this passage. In the parable of the Prodigal Son (Lk 15¹¹ᶠᶠ·), the farm-hands of the father are 'hired servants' in *RSV*, 'paid servants' in *NEB*. In America, 'hired men' would be a more familiar term for farm-hands than 'hired servants', and 'paid servants' would be quite intolerable; but would an English farmer, or his son, speak of the men who worked for him as 'paid servants?' In Luke 16¹, *NEB* speaks of 'a bailiff'; in America, the word is never used in the sense given to it here. We could build up an extensive glossary of terms that have come to have different meanings in the two areas. As 'Scoticisms', I might mention the use of 'ever' in such phrases as 'God knew his own before ever they were' (Rom 8²⁹); 'I hope to send (Timothy) as soon as ever I can see how things are going with me' (Phil 2²³); and the 'humble folk' of Romans 12¹⁶.

In its general character, this is a very free translation, sometimes going so far as to become paraphrase. Once it has been decided that the translation shall not be literal, it is always a question to know what degree of freedom may be permitted. The translators have defined their purpose for us in clear terms.

It should be said that our intention has been to offer a translation in the strict sense, and not a paraphrase, and we have not wished to encroach on the field of the commentator. But if the best commentary is a good translation, it is also true that every intelligent translation is in a sense a paraphrase. But if paraphrase means taking the liberty of introducing into a passage something which is not there, to elucidate the meaning which is there, it can be said that we have taken this liberty only with extreme caution, and in a very few passages, where without it we could see no way to attain our aim of making the meaning as clear as it could be made. Taken as a whole, our version claims to be a translation, free, it may be, rather than literal, but a faithful translation nevertheless, so far as we could compass it (p. x).

Taking the version as a whole, this claim is justified. There are a few instances, however, where we seem to be confronted with paraphrase rather than translation. I shall offer a few examples from the Fourth Gospel. In John 1^{12}, 'to those who have yielded him their allegiance' (literally, 'to those who believed on his Name')—surely this is periphrastic and interpretative. In 8^{31}, 'If you dwell within the revelation I have brought' (literally, 'If you abide in my word'); there is certainly a large measure of interpretation of the phrase 'in my word' when it is rendered 'within the revelation I have brought'—St John's Greek is as expandable as Monsieur Jourdain's Turkish. Or again, in 9^3, 'that God's power might be displayed in curing him' (literally, 'that the works of God might be made manifest in him'). The Greek text does not say, and does not even seem to imply, that the manifestation of the works of God is limited to the cure. It must be granted, however, that it is not often that the translators have gone as far as this by way of paraphrase. And these examples are not intended to suggest that the rendering of the Fourth Gospel is exceptionally free. On the contrary, it seems to me to be very faithful, for all its freedom; and it abounds in most felicitous phrases. The very great difficulties of translating the theological discourses of this Gospel, with their severe simplicity of wording combined with profundity and complexity of thought, have been brilliantly overcome. The dialogue—artificial as it nearly always is—is exceptionally well handled.

The desire to make the translation intelligible to the ordinary reader has led to the disappearance of any number of familiar theological terms—terms familiar to the churchman, that is to say. In Hebrews 10[19], it was impossible to avoid the expression, 'the blood of Jesus', since the whole argument revolves around the significance of blood in the sacrificial system of the old covenant; but in Romans 3[25], ἐν τῷ αὐτοῦ αἵματι is rendered not by the literal 'by (or, 'in') his blood', but by the interpretative phrase 'by his sacrificial death'; in Romans 5[9], we again have 'Christ's sacrificial death' in place of the literal 'by his blood'; but in 1 John 1[7] we have 'the blood of Jesus his Son'. 'Propitiation' is not used; in 1 John ἱλασμὸς περὶ τῶν ἁμαρτιῶν ἡμῶν is rendered 'the remedy for the defilement of our sins' (2[2], cf. 4[10]). In Romans 3[25], ἱλαστήριον is rendered 'the means of expiating sin'. 'Redeem' is used, but not (so far as I have observed) 'Redemption'. In Colossians 1[14], ἐν ᾧ ἔχομεν τὴν ἀπολύτρωσιν is rendered 'in whom our release is secured', and the same phrase is rendered in the same way in the parallel verse of Ephesians (1[7]); in Romans 3[24], for διὰ τῆς ἀπολυτρώσεως we have 'through his act of liberation'. ὀργή ('wrath') is generally rendered 'retribution'; thus in Romans 1[18] (ὀργὴ θεοῦ), we have 'divine retribution'; in 2[5] 'wrath against the day of wrath' becomes 'retribution for the day of retribution'; and in Romans 5[9] ἀπὸ τῆς ὀργῆς is rendered 'from final retribution'. In the report of the preaching of John the Baptist, 'the wrath to come' is translated as 'the coming retribution'; but in 1 Thessalonians 1[10], the equivalent phrase is given as 'the terrors of judgement to come'. In Colossians 3[6], ἡ ὀργὴ τοῦ θεοῦ is rendered 'God's dreadful judgement'. σωτήρ is rendered 'Saviour' in John 4[42]; but in Luke 2[11] and Philippians 3[20], it is 'deliverer'; in the Pastoral Epistles, 'Saviour' is used throughout. ἅγιοι is almost always rendered 'God's people' (even in Matthew 27[52]); in Romans 1[7], the phrase 'dedicated people' is used. The peculiar Pauline use of σάρξ offers difficulties. It is nearly always rendered 'our lower nature'. ἐν τῇ σαρκί (Rom 7[5]) becomes 'on the level of our lower nature'; τὸ φρόνημα τῆς σαρκός and its antithesis τὸ φρόνημα τοῦ πνεύματος (Rom 8[5, 6]) can only be managed by turning these two verses into the paraphrase: 'Those who live on the level of our lower nature have their outlook formed by it, and that spells death; but those who live on the level of the spirit have the spiritual outlook, and that is life and peace.' Similarly in verse 9 (following), with equally great freedom, ὑμεῖς δὲ οὐκ ἐστὲ ἐν σαρκὶ ἀλλ᾽ ἐν πνεύματι is rendered: 'But that is not how you live. You are on the spiritual level.' This treatment raises questions about the true understanding of Pauline anthropology. These renderings seem to imply that Paul thinks of human nature in itself as compounded of two elements, a higher and a lower; whereas it seems rather that for him 'the flesh' stands for the whole nature of man, until by the gift of God he receives the Spirit. I have an uneasy feeling that this very tempting rendering involves a theological misunderstanding of some magnitude (not that I would suggest that this was intended by the translators). In Philippians 3, σάρξ is rendered by 'anything external' (verse 3); 'externals' (verse 4)—but are the things of which Paul once was proud (descent, religious training, pious zeal, moral rectitude) properly classified as 'externals'?

The treatment of δικαιοσύνη calls for special attention—calls, indeed, for much more extended discussion than is possible in a review. Theological questions are involved here, inescapably. Before the translator can decide on his rendering, he must first of all come to some decision about the meaning of the word. But there is perhaps no phrase in the whole New Testament that carries greater theological weight (for all of us, at least, who acknowledge our debt to Martin Luther), or that offers more difficulty of interpretation than the words δικαιοσύνη θεοῦ. It is not simply a matter of finding an English counter to put in place of the Greek one. Even the Greek word δικαιοσύνη is not to be understood in purely Greek terms; the ten books of Plato's *Republic* are concerned with an inquiry into the meaning of δικαιοσύνη, and there is almost nothing in them that throws light upon the meaning of the word for St Paul. We have to go behind the Greek to the Hebrew, and even within the Hebrew of the Old Testament there is a considerable semantic development in the usage of the word. 'Justice', 'righteousness'—one of these words has to be used, in default of anything better; but neither of them carries the overtones of δικαιοσύνη nor do both in combination. δικαιοσύνη θεοῦ conveys also the thought of triumph—God's triumph over all that is hostile to him, over all that defiles his fair creation; of vindication— God's vindication of his own people against all their oppressors and accusers; of forgiveness—God's free forgiveness of the sins of those who cast themselves upon his mercy. And in St Paul, all these thoughts belong in an eschatological setting—in the framework of the Last Judgement, of the Day of Wrath which is for the redeemed the Day of Salvation. Such a word, such a complex of

thoughts in a single word, is the despair of translators; and in fact
no translation could of itself provide the reader with all that he
needs for understanding. The translators, faced with an insoluble
problem, have dealt with it valiantly. They have been bold
enough to have recourse to different renderings even within the
one passage, the classic exposition of the Gospel, in the opening
chapters of Romans. In 1¹⁷, we have, for δικαιοσύνη γὰρ θεοῦ ἐν
αὐτῷ ἀποκαλύπτεται, the rendering: 'because here is revealed God's
way of righting wrong.' In 3²¹, for δικαιοσύνη θεοῦ πεφανέρωται we
have 'God's justice has been brought to light', followed in verse 22
by 'it is God's way of righting wrong' (again translating δικαιοσύνη
θεοῦ). In verse 25, 'God meant by this to demonstrate his justice'
(for εἰς ἔνδειξιν τῆς δικαιοσύνης αὐτοῦ), and the same phrase is
repeated in verse 26. Then in 4³, the faith of Abraham 'was
counted to him as righteousness' (ἐλογίσθη αὐτῷ εἰς δικαιοσύνην);
and in verse 11, circumcision is 'the hallmark of the righteousness
(σφραγῖδα τῆς δικαιοσύνης) which faith had given him when he
was still uncircumcised'. (Some question might be raised about the
anachronistic 'hallmark'.) The adjective δίκαιος is nearly always
rendered 'just' or 'just man'; in the Habakkuk quotation of 1¹⁷ it is
rendered 'is justified'. The verb δικαιόω is always rendered by
'justify', except in the quotation of 3⁴ (from Ps 51), where 'vindicate' is used; and—much more striking—in 4⁵, where ἐπὶ τὸν
δικαιοῦντα τὸν ἀσεβῆ is rendered with great boldness: 'in him who
acquits the guilty' (cf. 8³³, 'pronounces acquittal'). This seems
to overdo the paradox, and to go somewhat beyond the literal sense
of 'in him who justifies the impious'; in any case, if δικαιόω means
simply 'acquit' here, why would the same rendering not serve also
in 3²⁶, ²⁸, and ³⁰? All through this argument, the question is how
far we should go in insisting on the 'forensic' sense of this verb.
My own feeling is that while the forensic sense lies in the background, the verb is being somewhat forced into a context for which
it is not entirely fitted, where it comes to mean virtually 'forgive'.
I suspect that St Paul would have been profoundly shocked at
finding his words taken to mean that 'God acquits the guilty'.
Certainly his use of the quotation from Psalm 32 (in 4⁷, ⁸) is only
comprehensible on the supposition that he takes δικαιοῦν τὸν
ἀσεβῆ, ἀφιέναι τὰς ἀνομίας, ἐπικαλύπτειν τὰς ἁμαρτίας and
ἁμαρτίαν οὐ λογίζεσθαι to be virtually equivalent expressions. For
all that, the translation of this very difficult section of Romans is

admirable. It goes as far as translation could possibly go to make the thought of the apostle intelligible to English readers.

Within this area, there is something particularly intriguing about the decision of the translators to use the phrase 'God's justice', in place of the 'righteousness of God'. The Latin Vulgate rendering is '*justitia Dei*', and in keeping with this, Roman Catholic translations and Roman Catholic commentators and theologians have consistently adopted the English rendering: 'the justice of God'. It is probable that in earlier English (non-Roman) versions, the rendering 'righteousness of God' has reflected Luther's '*Gottes Gerechtigkeit*'. The theological consequences flowing from this difference of phrasing in translation have been incalculably great. The adoption of the rendering 'justice' in the new translation is of course not an indication of Romanizing tendencies among the translators (though some fools and fanatics are sure to make this accusation), but it may perhaps be taken as a symbol of the fact that discussion of the theological truth of 'Justification by Faith' is no longer on the same ground as it was in the disputations of the sixteenth century. That ground has been cut from under the feet of Romanists and Protestants alike by modern study of the Septuagintal and Hebraic background of St Paul's theological vocabulary. . . .

It is hard to avoid feeling that there is no small degree of temerity in the attempt of a single scholar to pass in review the carefully polished work of a large group of distinguished and highly competent colleagues, which they have published after many years of labour. It is probable that almost every point that I have raised has been the subject of discussion among them. This review may perhaps leave the impression that there is much to find fault with in this translation. I must therefore make it clear that the more I work with it, the more I find to admire. Certainly it fulfils its primary aims of accuracy and clarity; it brings the New Testament writings to people in the language of today. More than that, it achieves in its chosen idiom something of unmistakable literary distinction. It makes an immediate impression of vigour; it arrests the reader at once, and brings the challenge of the Gospel before him with fresh insistence. The translators have put us all in their debt, and their accomplishment is worthy of all our praise.

Catholic Biblical Quarterly[1]

RAYMOND E. BROWN, s.s.

...IN EVALUATING this monumental work, we shall begin with a question of principle. In our language where the AV has had such literary influence, a new translation always raises a problem of advisability. Personally, having once paid tribute to the recognized place of the AV in the English language, this reviewer is wholeheartedly in sympathy with the effort of a new translation. There is a point beyond which the revision of revisions ceases to have meaning. With all the effort expended in the American production of the *RSV*, the British would have been foolish to produce yet another revision. The laments for the familiar terms and poetic balance of the AV are, in our opinion, somewhat vain— familiarity would soon disappear if people stop reading the Bible, and that would certainly happen unless the Bible be put into more understandable English. T. S. Eliot is not far from the truth when he says: 'Those who talk of the Bible as a "monument of English prose" are merely admiring it as a monument over the grave of Christianity.'

This said, we may now turn to evaluating the modern style of the *NEB*; the reactions have been mixed: some have found the *NEB* still somewhat stilted; others have ranted against its modernity, even subjecting it to the slanderous indignity of referring to it as 'a beatnik bible'. This reviewer finds the charge of extreme modernity ridiculous: on the whole the translation is in sober modern English, and avoids the extremes of familiar speech. (There are what might be considered occasional lapses, e.g. 2 Corinthians 12[13]: 'I never sponged upon you.') Complaints about such points as the use of 'girls' instead of 'virgins' in the parable about the wise and foolish (Mt 25[1]) reflect little knowledge of the Semitic idiom underlying the Greek. If anything, we would tend to find the English a bit too staid. Of course, allowance must be made for the fact that we are dealing with British English which

[1] Vol. XXIII (July 1961), pp. 321-4.

does sound formal to American ears. For instance, in John 5 we hear that the darkness has never *quenched* the light; in John 2¹⁰ the steward *hails* the bridegroom instead of calling to him; John 16²³ reads: 'If you ask the Father for anything in my name, he will give it you.' These examples, chosen at random, could scarcely be considered everyday English for an American. Beyond regional differences, however, there is one question of usage which is more general. In the *NEB* 'Thou' is employed in addressing God the Father; thus, John 17²: 'For thou hast made him sovereign over all mankind, to give eternal life to all whom thou hast given him.' There is room for difference of opinion on this point; but personally we feel that it fits very awkwardly into a modern translation, and we do not see any insult to the Divinity in employing 'You' as a form of address (as does the Confraternity Version of the OT).

We now come to the question of the fidelity of the translation to the original. Necessarily an attempt to put the Bible into modern idiom must employ a certain freedom of translation. As a result, the *NEB* is much freer than the *RSV* (which gives the *RSV* a certain advantage for class-room use); in the style of its translation it is closer to the Goodspeed NT. On the whole, the freedom of translation catches quite well the meaning intended in the original. Occasionally the *NEB* adds clarifying words (although without any indication that the additions are not in the original). For instance, Romans 5¹⁵ reads: 'But *God's* act of grace is out of all proportion to *Adam's* wrongdoing'. (Italics are ours to indicate additions.) The Petrine promise (Mt 16¹⁸) is rendered: 'You are Peter, *the Rock*; and on this rock I will build my church.' Such additions are obviously only clarifications, but some might prefer to have indicated that they are additions.

The real danger in the direction of freedom is that of paraphrase and over-interpretative translation. In general, the *NEB* avoids paraphrase (as some of the recent one-man translations do not). But one might wonder why so often an explanatory phrase has to be employed to translate what could be done by one word. In Romans 5¹⁴ we have: '. . . those who had not sinned as Adam did, by *disobeying a direct command*'—the words we have italicized translate παράβασις, which means 'transgression'. As to what constitutes an over-interpretative translation, there will be many opinions. We shall give a few examples where the *NEB* may be open to that accusation. In the famous passage, Mark 4¹¹ (*RSV:*

'For those outside everything is in parables; so that (ἵνα) they may indeed see but not perceive'), the *NEB* translates the ἵνα by 'so that' (as the Scripture says), although in the parallel in Luke 8[10] the same ἵνα is translated simply, 'in order that'. Many do hold that the ἵνα in Mark refers to a necessity of fulfilling the Scripture, but should this interpretation become part of the translation? 2 Thessalonians 2[7] reads in a literal translation: 'The mystery of lawlessness is already at work; only when he who now restrains is got out of the way, then will the lawless one be revealed.' The *NEB* gives us: 'For already the secret power of wickedness is at work, secret only for the present until the Restrainer disappears from the scene. And then he will be revealed, that wicked man. . . .' The shifting of the adverb ἄρτι ('now, for the present') from the subordinate clause to the main clause helps the interpretation of μυστήριον as 'secret power', and so does the insertion of the additional adjective 'secret'; but is this not a bit more interpretative than a translation should be?

At times, too, in our opinion the freedom of translation mars the theological intent of the NT writer. We all know how important is the concept of Jesus's name in John. Is it wise, then, to translate τοῖς πιστεύουσιν εἰς τὸ ὄνομα αὐτοῦ (1[12]) as 'to those who have yielded him their allegiance'? Many see a theological connection between the woman at Cana and the woman of Ap 12; but this is lost in translating the γύναι of 2[4] as 'mother' ('Your concern, mother, is not mine'). There is no evidence of a son addressing his mother as γύναι; if John wanted Mary called 'mother', would he not have used the precise Greek word for 'mother'?

In matters of textual freedom, the *NEB* follows a relatively sober standard. Alternate readings are found in footnotes with the indication: 'Some witnesses read. . . .' The Western non-interpolations in the last chapters of Luke are put into footnotes, but not the 'angel verses' of the Gethsemane scene (22[43-4]). The adulteress story in John is printed at the end of the Gospel. Mark 16[9-20] is separated from verse 8 but printed in the same type. Not as much as one might wish is made of recent textual studies on shorter readings in John, readings based on patristic evidence; but we are happy to see John 1[34] appear as 'This is God's Chosen One', and John 7[37-8] split into two parallel members: 'If anyone is thirsty let him come to me; whoever believes in me, let him drink.'

In format, while there are spacings in the text, there is a minimum of titles. This reviewer has been spoiled by the attractiveness of the Confraternity Version, with its abundance of titles. He believes that such helps are essential to the ordinary reader, as are introductions and an abundance of explanatory footnotes, both of which are lacking in the *NEB*. Of course, because of the number of religious denominations represented in the panels of translators, common agreement on the content of such helps may not have been possible. What is more, the most glaring omission in the *NEB*, in this reviewer's opinion, is the failure to employ poetic format for poetry such as that found in the Prologue of John, many speeches in John, a doxology such as that found at the end of Romans, etc. The *NEB* does print as poetry some of the Pauline hymns and the citations of OT poetry, but this is too limited. The Bible of Jerusalem is much better in this feature.

We have tried in this review to point out some of the difficulties to be encountered in reading the *NEB*. But we would not wish to leave the reader with an overall unfavourable impression. The *NEB* is infinitely more readable for the ordinary Christian than the AV or even the *RSV*. It is scientifically done and should lead many to an intelligent understanding of the message of Christ. The translators of the *NEB* are to be congratulated for their endurance in a long and arduous task (not eased by the tortures of committee work); their translation is a major contribution in Englishing God's word.

Christianity Today[1]

F. F. BRUCE

... A USEFUL SAMPLE

THE PROLOGUE to John's Gospel in the *NEB* will provide a useful sample. ...

The older versions present us with a word-for-word rendering of verse 1 of this chapter: 'In the beginning was the Word, and the Word was with God, and the Word was God.' The new version presents us with a 'meaning-for-meaning' rendering; that is to say, the translators have asked themselves, 'What does this sentence mean?' and have then set themselves to express that meaning in the best English they could find for the purpose. What is meant by the clause: 'In the beginning was the Word'? 'In the beginning' is probably a deliberate echo on the Evangelist's part of the opening words of the book of Genesis. At that time, he wishes us to understand, when God created heaven and earth, the Word through whom He created them was already in existence. The new translators have conveyed the Evangelist's purpose clearly by their rendering: 'When all things began, the Word already was.' Whether the echo of Genesis 1[1] will be as clear in the *New English Bible* as it is in the older versions we cannot say until we see the Old Testament part of the work and examine its rendering of Genesis 1[1]—and that will not be for some years yet.

The second clause of John 1[1] does not call for comment here, but the third clause makes us stop and think. 'The Word was God' is the old-established translation of this clause, and evangelicals have been at pains to defend this translation against such forms as 'the Word was divine' (which says less than the Evangelist intended) or even 'the Word was a god' (which says something quite different from what the Evangelist intended). Is the Evangelist's meaning better expressed by the *New English Bible*? 'What God was, the Word was' could be ambiguous out of its context; for example, in terms of classical Christian orthodoxy it might be said that God

[1] Vol. V, No. 12 (13th March 1961), pp. 5 (493)–8 (496).

was Father, Son, and Holy Spirit; but clearly it is not true that the Word was Father, Son, and Holy Spirit. In the context, however, the statement that 'what God was, the Word was' means that the Word was the perfect expression of all that God was—an idea which is repeated in several forms throughout the Gospel. That is what the new translators take the Evangelist to mean, I think, and that is what they intend to convey; but I am not sure that their intention will be immediately obvious to all readers. Prebendary J. B. Phillips has another way of rendering the same basic sense: 'At the beginning God expressed himself. That personal expression, that word, was with God, and was God, and he existed from God from the beginning.' At the crucial point this rendering retains the statement that the Word or self-expression of God 'was God'; and something may still be said on behalf of a rendering which keeps closer to a word-for-word translation here. There is, at any rate, no ground for thinking that the *New English Bible* has weakened the force of John's witness; the translators would agree with Professor C. K. Barrett that 'John intends that the whole of his gospel shall be read in the light of this verse. The deeds and words of Jesus are the deeds and words of God; if this be not true the book is blasphemous.'

The next thing that we notice in the *NEB* rendering of the Johannine prologue is that the translators have adopted the punctuation at the end of verse 3 which the revisers of 1881, 1901, and 1952 recorded in the margin. This punctuation, which has strong and early support, puts a period after 'was not anything made', and begins the next sentence: 'That which hath been made was life in him.' This is the construction which the *NEB* renders: 'All that came to be was alive with his life.' Here the crucial question is one of punctuation more than translation and on the whole the punctuation adopted in the text of *KJV*, RV, *ASV* and *RSV* seems preferable. The words as thus punctuated are translated in the margin of the *NEB*: 'no single created thing came into being without him. There was life in him . . .' (It may well be that this is the punctuation personally preferred by Professor C. H. Dodd, director of the *NEB* translation; at least this is what one could infer from a passage on page 318 of his book *The Interpretation of the Fourth Gospel*. But if that is so, it simply indicates that the new translation is a true joint-production, and that even the preference of the director could be outvoted.)

The remainder of the prologue illustrates the care which the translators have taken to express the full meaning of their text, and the considerable success which they have achieved. The rendering of John the Baptist's testimony in verse 15 shows up clearly the two senses in which 'before' is used (*KJV*, 'preferred before me, for he was before me'), and makes the emphasis on our Lord's pre-existence as unmistakable as could be desired. . . .

WHAT OF PROPITIATION?

At the beginning of 1961 a specimen page of the new translation was widely published, reproducing the first chapter of 1 John and a few verses of the second chapter. Special attention was directed by many readers to the rendering of 1 John 2^2, where the word 'propitiation', appearing here in *KJV*, RV and *ASV*, is not replaced by 'expiation', as in *RSV*, but by a fuller phrase: 'He is himself the remedy for the defilement of our sins, not our sins only but the sins of all the world'. In recent years there has been considerable discussion about the true meaning of the words which the older versions of the New Testament translate by 'propitiation'; and in this discussion Professor Dodd himself has played an outstanding part. The term 'propitiation' disappears from the *NEB*. In 1 John 4^{10} the Father is spoken of as 'sending the Son as the remedy for the defilement of our sins'. In Hebrews 2^{17} Christ is qualified as 'high priest before God, to expiate the sins of the people'. In Romans 3^{25} similarly 'God designed him to be the means of expiating sin by his sacrificial death'. The replacement of 'propitiation' by other expressions might be justified on the ground that nowadays it is a technical theological term, not readily understood —in its biblical sense at least—by the majority of English speakers. In that case the translators might well endeavour to express its biblical sense by other means, and in the two passages in 1 John they have succeeded reasonably well in doing this. The statement that Christ is 'the remedy for the defilement of our sins', while it may not convey with complete precision the sense of the Greek word ἱλασμός, does make two positive points—that sin is a defilement from which we need to be cleansed, and that Christ is 'God's remedy for sin'. But it does not appear that 'expiate' and 'expiation' are a substantial improvement on 'propitiate' and 'propitiation', either idiomatically or theologically. It is true that the Greek words so translated have a meaning in the Bible different from that which they have in pagan literature; their biblical meaning has been conditioned by their biblical context, in which 'propitiation' is something which God himself provides for sinners. But if the Greek words have had their meaning conditioned by their biblical context, why can we not understand the English terms 'propitiate' and 'propitiation' as equally conditioned? According to the *NEB*, 'God's wrath rests upon him' who disobeys the Son (Jn 3³⁶), and 'we see divine retribution revealed from heaven and falling upon all the godless wickedness of men' (Rom 1¹⁸). This wrath or retribution is God's 'strange work' (Isa 28²¹), something not congenial to his nature as is the mercy in which he delights; but when it rests upon men or falls upon their godless wickedness, how is it to be removed? This is the question which is answered by the statement in Romans 3²⁵ that God has appointed Christ to be a ἱλαστήριον 'by his sacrificial death'. We require a rendering of ἱλαστήριον which brings this fact out, while emphasizing that it is God who provides it.

Nothing is easier, however, than to pick out renderings from a new translation and suggest that the sense might have been better expressed. The New Testament panel of translators are to be congratulated on the excellence of their achievement. It is not the reviews which appear on publication day or the day after that will decide the acceptance of the new version. That will be decided, over the months and years that lie ahead, by the people for whom it was prepared. We trust with the translators, 'that under the providence of Almighty God this translation may open the truth of the scriptures to many who have been hindered in their approach to it by barriers of language'.

Theology Today[1]

HENRY J. CADBURY

...IT WILL be in order to make some comments about each of the major areas in which the procedure of the new translation can be illustrated.

GREEK TEXT

When the Revised Version of 1881 was made in England, one scholar, F. J. A. Hort, was the most influential in the matter of text. The printed text that goes under his name and Westcott's was practically the same as that of the Revisers. This was of course a great advance over the late and few MSS behind the printed editions available in 1611. Today textual knowledge is more widespread and valuable sources are more numerous so that a team of translators can discuss the questions as peers yet with continued uncertainty. Apparently variant readings were dealt with simply in their places. This is not to say decisions were made *ad hoc* or that an eclectic text was created. In many respects we are in our knowledge of text much where we were last century in spite of the newly discovered early papyri—some as extensive as the Bodmer John and the Beatty Paul.

The notes, which run uniformly: 'Some witnesses read (add, etc.)', call attention to passages where the British scholars felt alternative readings sufficiently important to indicate both. Besides choosing these passages, and they are not numerous (there are 27 in Matthew, 54 in Luke, 37 in Acts, to mention only the three longest books) it was necessary to select the most probable one for the text and to place the alternate or alternates in the margin. Without going into detail I would say that the choices show often heavy dependence on the evidence of Marcion and the early church fathers or versions as commending readings not too well attested by Greek manuscripts. The cases where 'one witness' is regarded as having a reading worth mention in the notes or

[1] Vol. XVIII, No. 2 (July 1961), pp. 188–200.

adoption in the text are not usually Codex Vaticanus or the new papyri.[2] There is no conspicuous tendency to give greater value than in the past to the Western Text but cf. Mark 1[41] text, Luke 11[42] mg., 12[14] mg., 12[27] text, Acts 20[4] text. Many of the most famous Western variants are not noted at all.

THE GREEK VOCABULARY

There are few comments needed under this score. At least once we are told in the notes that 'the Greek is obscure' (Mk 14[41]), and again that 'the meaning of the Greek word is uncertain' (Acts 23[23]). But I take it that the same is true of other words or phrases. In fact more than half of the footnotes, introduced by 'Or', required, as with textual variants, a choice of such cases to be mentioned, and an allocation to text and note respectively of the preferred and the less preferred alternative. I suppose this may be the first of the standard English versions to suggest even in the notes the proposed meanings of 'what you can afford' for $\tau \grave{\alpha}$ $\dot{\epsilon}\nu\acute{o}\nu\tau\alpha$ in Luke 11[41], 'within your grasp' for $\dot{\epsilon}\nu\tau\grave{o}s$ $\dot{\upsilon}\mu\hat{\omega}\nu$ in Luke 17[21], and 'do not use vessels in common' at John 4[9] (text) for $o\dot{\upsilon}$ $\sigma\upsilon\gamma\chi\rho\hat{\omega}\nu\tau\alpha\iota$.[3] At Luke 15[13] 'turned into cash' was anticipated by Moffatt. But I miss in text or notes the suggestion at Acts 9[34] '*has* healed' and at Hebrews 11[27] (with W. Bauer) 'he kept his eyes constantly upon him who is unseen'.

There still remain many uncertainties, many more than even the notes suggest. Thus at Philippians 4[8] neither the text 'gracious' nor the note 'of good repute' exhausts the quite plausible alternatives here of the single Greek adjective $\epsilon\ddot{\upsilon}\phi\eta\mu os$. In this area of semantics, however, unless I have overlooked some flagrant errors, the translation is on firm ground, and shows marks of real competence. Even when one disagrees with a rendering, its reasonableness is hard to deny. It should be remembered that in Greek the indicative and imperative are often identical and so are the interrogative and declarative. And of course modern quotation marks

[2] The 'one witness' mentioned at Matthew 1[16] is the Sinaitic Syriac, at 6[28] an obscured first-hand reading of Codex Sinaiticus, at Mark 1[41] mg. two old Latin MSS, at John 19[29] codex 476*, at Revelation 2[22] mg. the Armenian (?). At Luke 11[33] the text is supported by only the Beatty papyrus and a few other witnesses, and at Hebrews 12[1] another Beatty papyrus is the one witness which reads: 'The sin which all too readily distracts us.' At Acts 10[19] mg. the one witness is Codex Vaticanus.

[3] For the last two see respectively *Harvard Theol. Review*, XLI (1948). 1–8, and later articles, and *Journal of Biblical Literature*, LXIX (1950), pp. 137–47.

and the use of capitals require decisions not obvious in the non-committal Greek. Consistency in the latter (as e.g. in Gospel—gospel; Sabbath—sabbath; Spirit—spirit) is hard to attain. And as for the Holy Spirit, the Greek frequently gives us no clue as to whether we should call it 'he' or call him 'it'. In John 7^{39} 'which' is used, but in the Comforter passages in the later chapters of John (here translated 'Advocate') 'he' and 'whom' are employed. So 'he', 'himself' in Paul. The problem is sidestepped, skilfully at Acts 5^{32} 'the Holy Spirit given by God', but not so skilfully at Romans 5^5 'through the Holy Spirit he has given us'. For the beast in Revelation 'it (its)' is consistently used now. The *King James Version*, which never employs 'its' anyhow, had always 'his' and 'him'.

Conversely a distinction which the Greek does make in pronouns is obscured by English 'you' for both singular and plural. This distinction is lost in passages like much of Matthew 6. At Luke 22^{31} 'all of you', and in Acts 25^{26} and in the letters to individuals 'you all', unlike its American singular use, shows where the plural is meant. As in other modern translations 'thou' is used only in address to God. With it are the verb forms 'wilt', 'dost', 'hadst', etc., and 'thee' and 'thy'. Even 'thine' is used before 'h' or vowels, 'thine own' (Jn 17^5), 'thine altars' (Rom 11^3) but also 'thy house' (Jn 2^{17}), 'thy hands' (Heb 1^{10}), 'thy enemies', 'thy footstool' (Heb 1^{13}, cf. Mk 12^{36} and parallels, 'your enemies', 'your footstool'), and never 'mine' before vowels but always 'my own', 'my account', 'my angels', etc. . . .

THE ENGLISH RENDERING

This is a major problem of any translation. At most I can deal with a few general and specific problems. The manner of translating explained on p. ix of the Introduction is particularly evident in the Pauline epistles, and involves breaking up long sentences into short ones, dividing relative clauses into separate statements, rearranging clauses and even smaller units. One device frequently employed throughout is the repetition of a word in rather loose sentence structure. One can have no quarrel with such rearrangements as place the first person after nouns or pronouns of other persons as in English idiom, e.g. John 2^4, 'Your concern, mother, is not mine' (AV, 'what have I to do with thee ?'); 10^{30}, 'my Father and I'; in 1 Corinthians 4^6, 'Apollos and myself'; in 1 Corinthians 9^6,

Galatians 2⁹, 'Barnabas and I (myself)'. In Revelation, 'hot and cold', 'great and small', 'slave and free', 'bride and bridegroom' are apparently adjudged to be more natural English order than their opposites when the latter occur in the Greek. But in Paul 'slave and free' is retained at Galatians 3²⁸ and reversed at Colossians 3¹¹. 'Day and night' is the regular sequence in the Greek of Revelation and is retained in the English. 'Night and day' is the order in the epistles and is also retained there. But when it occurs in Luke-Acts it has been transposed. A longer reversal is 'year and month', 'day and hour' (Rev 9¹⁵).

In the Greek NT Priscilla is mentioned before her husband twice out of three occurrences both in Paul and (except the Western text) in Acts. This is kept in the *NEB*. So in the case of a somewhat different matter of sequence, 'Christ Jesus', found in Paul and some other writings, the translators retain the order where they find it, as they do 'Jesus Christ' when it occurs. Since the reason for this variation is obscure, so unevenly distributed but related apparently to case or construction, they had little other option.

There can be little objection to 'adding' words in translation if they are really needed. In the following passage from the beginning of Revelation that qualification may be queried of the words in italics which are not in the Greek (italics are not employed by the *NEB*):

Happy is the man who reads, and happy those who listen to the words of *this* prophecy and heed what is written in it. For the hour *of fulfilment* is near.

John to the seven churches in *the province* of Asia. . . .

To him who loves us and freed us from our sins with his *life's* blood, who made of us a royal house, *to serve* as the priests of his God and Father—to him *be* glory and dominion for ever and ever! Amen.

Behold, he is coming with the clouds! Every eye shall see him, and *among them* those who pierced him; and all the peoples of the world shall lament *in remorse*. So it shall be. Amen.

Actually I suppose one of the words added most often in this translation without the corresponding Greek is 'God'. This was practised in one expression of the *King James Version* which regularly rendered the strong negative μὴ γένοιτο[3] by 'God for-bid'. Of such locutions in the new version the regular use of 'God's people' for οἱ ἅγιοι ('the saints') is one of the most frequent and noticeable. In Galatians alone the word 'God' is added in the English at 1[15]; 2[2, 8]; 3[5]; 4[23, 28]; 5[4, 8, 10]; and 6[14].

The use of two nouns for one in the Greek is understandable when διάνοια is rendered at Colossians 1[21] 'heart and mind' or when 'limb(s) and organ(s)' translates μέλος (-η) at Romans 12[4, 5]; 1 Corinthians 12[12, 18]; but at Luke 16[17] the phrase 'one dot or stroke' seems too full for the single μίαν κεραίαν, cf. Matthew 5[18], 'not a letter, not a stroke', for ἰῶτα ἓν ἢ μία κεραία. At 1 Timothy 3[2] the double rendering 'our leader or bishop' looks like a com-promise of controversy within the panel of translators.

Less conspicuous I think are the kinds of situation where a Greek word is omitted in the *New English Bible*. Greek authors still in the first century AD generally maintained the classical custom of beginning with a connective particle or avoiding asyndeton. Hence one of the commonest omissions in *NEB* is initial 'And' (καί or postpositive δέ). And another use of καί is with equal propriety unrepresented in the English. That is when it appears in a relative clause or in the apodosis of a condition. The *King James Version* over-translated it in such instances by 'also', as 'who also betrayed him', 'which also they did', 'whom also he named apostles'. Examples of its appropriate omission after an 'if' clause will be found in 2 Timothy 2[11, 12].

The translators explain that they deliberately vary the English equivalents of the same Greek word. There are legitimate reasons for doing so. The original has more than one nuance and not in every occurrence does the same English satisfy. The variation can be made simply to avoid monotonous repetition. But the practice has its drawbacks. It obscures the actual repetition of the original, both when that was intentional and when it is a mark of the author's indifference to recurrence. For the former I cite the repetition in 2 Corinthians 1 and 7 of the word for 'comfort', noun and verb. But *NEB* uses for the verb, 'comfort', and for the cognate noun, 'consolation'. For the latter phenomenon note the repetition in Mark 12[41-4] of βάλλω ('cast', six times) and γαζοφυλάκιον

---

[3] The skill in variation is well exemplified by the renderings of this single phrase: 'God forbid!'; 'By no means'; 'Of course not'; 'Certainly not!'; 'No, no!'; 'Never!'; 'Far from it!' 'No, never!'; 'I cannot believe it!'

('treasury', three times). The *NEB* has for the first, 'drop', twice, 'give', four times, for the other, 'chest', twice. They were perhaps unconsciously following the example of Luke in 21[1-4], who made similar and other improvements of Mark.

This practice of *NEB* means, as it meant in *KJV*, that in parallel passages, synoptic or otherwise, the reader cannot trust the English text to indicate faithfully the degree of likeness and difference between the parallels. Evidently attention was paid to this difficult matter, but in places the English is unnecessarily more identical or less identical than the Greek, e.g. in parallels between Luke and Matthew and between Ephesians and Colossians. (Jesus) Bar-Abbas in Matthew over against Barabbas in the other gospels is a noticeable case. In two gospels 'a cock crew', in two 'the cock crew'.

In different contexts one can understand variant English for the same Greek word, e.g. 'pigeons' of the temple and its market, 'doves' elsewhere. But why in a genuinely new translation unless under the influence of the King James and earlier Protestant versions is 'whore' used only in Revelation, elsewhere 'harlot' or 'prostitute' for the same Greek word?

Understandable but not therefore justifiable is the sensitivity with which some readers will scrutinize the translation of certain religious terms—whether ecclesiastical or theological. We may be sure that not doctrinal prejudice but some good reason lies behind the careful choices the translators have made. We have already mentioned one such: 'God's people.' This, except at Matthew 27[52], means what we would call 'Christians'. That too is a term used much more frequently in English, including Paul's letters, than the Greek word that it transliterates is in Greek text. And in all three instances of the Greek (Acts 11[26]; 26[28]; 1 Pet 4[16]) there is a nuance or even a dating for the word that its wider currency in *NEB* seems to ignore. 'Christian' is also used as an adjective, for example in 1 Timothy, 'Christian faith', 'Christian brothers', 'non-Christian public'. To be able to speak of Jewish Christians, Gentile Christians, fellow Christians, or Christian brothers is a great convenience for the translator; so too the Christian movement for 'the way'. Several other new words for members of the Christian movement or fellow believers are used, like (God's) dedicated people, one of our company, comrade, comrade-in-arms, the brotherhood, and most original of all the adjectival 'incorporate in Christ', at the beginning of several of Paul's epistles (cf. Rom 6[5], 'incorporate with him'). Paul's phrase 'in Christ' in other connections has required resourceful ingenuity to render. But in the gospels Christ is mostly translated by 'Messiah'. This I suppose was an attempt to avoid anachronism. But where Christ may be thought of as parallel to pagan saviours the word used for Him is 'deliverer' (Lk 2[11]; Phil 3[20]); but in John 4[42]; 1 John 4[14], 'Saviour (or saviour) of the world'.

The local church is regularly called congregation or community. It may include individuals called deacon (but not deaconess), elder and bishop. The first day of the week is simply Sunday. Beside the day of Pentecost there is Whitsuntide (1 Cor 16[8]). At the last supper when a blessing is said and a hymn sung these are 'the blessing' and 'the Passover hymn'.

Such details do not do justice to the evident care to deal with general problems wisely. The rendering of $\pi\hat{a}s$ ('all'), extensive with abstract nouns, shows it and so does the treatment of the word $\sigma\acute{a}\rho\xi$ ('flesh'). A study of the occurrences of this word would be a good example of the variety and resourcefulness of the translators. It is only one of the ancient physiological idioms that are not meaningful when literally translated. Since this and heart and bosom and face and bowels are so understandingly dealt with, one regrets that the passage about the single and evil eye was not as masterfully and freely translated. I should commend for study the renderings of $\H{o}\sigma\iota os$ or $\sigma\epsilon\mu\nu\acute{o}s$ and their derivatives. Where I am puzzled by an item I am prepared to reserve judgement and to assume that there are good reasons. But the reasons are mostly transparent if one has studied the passage with care.

Here are examples of treatment of famously difficult passages:

Matthew 26[25] *et al.*, The words are yours [margin: *Or* It is as you say].

Acts 26[28], You think it will not take much to win me over and make a Christian of me.

Romans 1[17] *et al.*, He shall gain life who is justified through faith (Hebrews 10[38] . . . and by faith my righteous servant shall find life.)

1 Corinthians 15[8], In the end he appeared even to me; though this birth of mine was monstrous (with inversion of clauses in the sequel).

2 Corinthians 5[16], With us therefore worldly standards have ceased to count in our estimate of any man; even if once they counted in our understanding of Christ, they do so now no longer.

Philippians 2[5-7] (with alternatives in the notes to two of the phrases), Let your bearing towards one another arise out of your life in Christ Jesus. For the divine nature was his from the first; yet he did not think to snatch at equality with God.

1 Timothy 3[12], A deacon must be faithful to his one wife [Or married to one wife, or married only once]. Similarly 3[2]; Titus 1[6]; and (without any note) 1 Timothy 5[9].

Among those who will welcome parts of this new version are those who without benefit of any knowledge of the original feel confident of their own ability to tell a translator what the original must mean and like Job's 'comforters' accuse the older translators of 'speaking unrighteously for God'. No phrase has seemed to these persons more improper than the prayer to God to 'lead us not into temptation'. Such intuitive correction had changed God to Satan when the Chronicler wrote, 'Satan provoked David to number Israel' for 'God moved David' (2 Samuel), or when James wrote, 'Let no man say when he is tempted I am tempted of God, for God . . . does not tempt any man', or when the Lord's prayer was rendered by Torrey 'let us not yield to temptation' or by Lamsa 'do not let us enter into temptation', a translation which claiming the *Peshitta* as original did much to commend his version to laymen in spite of its completely erroneous hypothesis of the relation of Greek and Syriac. The present translators evidently with good conscience render, 'And do not bring us to the test', though they follow (in Matthew) with the wording: 'But save us from the evil one', and keep the word 'temptation' in James.

Even more striking and welcome to some theological preference is the almost complete omission of the phrase 'wrath [ὀργή] (of God)'. This is not because it is anthropopathic (cf. 'love') or because wrath is obsolescent or archaic in English. It is used in John 3[36] ('God's wrath') and Revelation 19[15] for θυμός, and 'anger' is a natural personal substitute. The translators prefer 'retribution' or 'divine retribution' in Paul, 'judgement' in Ephesians (Colossians), 'vengeance' in Revelation. What is in effect a justification of this interpretation appears by coincidence in the recent publication of the Presidential Address of S.N.T.S. by G. H. C. Macgregor.[4]

THE GENERAL STYLE OF ENGLISH

Obviously this translation succeeds generally in avoiding archaic English, as it aimed to do. Its phrasing is often fresh and idiomatic as well as felicitous in sound and faithful to the original meaning. One cannot criticize occasional and restricted freedom to paraphrase. The translators speak of their English as timeless. That is a courageous claim, if it refers not to the past but to the present and the future. Here again only the past is secure. Can one claim in either language or belief *quod semper, quod ubique, quod ab omnibus?* Each reader will have his instances of doubt as well as of assent. Perhaps what seems unfamiliar in America is current in England. . . .

The frustrations which translators must feel amid their difficult devices deserve our sympathy. Besides those mentioned before, they include the question, When does legitimate variety become illegitimate inconsistency? In the choice of general level of English there is also a dilemma. If the wording is fresh, contemporary, and idiomatic it will make the text not only understandable but natural and vivid. At the same time it will obscure the fact that these are ancient minds of a different world or mentality from our own. Perhaps the reader is kept aware of this better by more formal, not to say archaic, style. To keep a translation life-like but also true to antiquity and history is to combine two almost incompatible aims. In an unexpected way the old *King James Version* has come in time to fulfil one of them and to sacrifice the other. It remains to be seen and felt whether the new translation merely reverses the imbalance.

Such delicate choices—archaizing *versus* modernizing—will have an unconscious reaction from lay readers. The *New English Bible*, as did the *King James* itself, at first, will meet objection just because it is new. Let us hope that its critics will not add the quite irrelevant prejudices—ecclesiastical, economic, and political—displayed by some opponents of the *RSV* in America. Perhaps the fact that this version is not officially tied to any National Council of Churches or as promptly subjected to the guilt by association technique will exempt it from some unworthy fault-finding even in America. What indirect motives for criticism it may have to

4 *New Testament Studies*, VII (1961), 101–10.

face in its own market cannot be predicted. It deserves well of its own people. Twenty years ago during the Battle of Britain, Churchill's words about the Royal Air Force became a favourite slogan: 'Never did so many owe so much to so few.' As millions of copies of this product of the little group of scholarly translators are circulated and read by their eager fellow countrymen, the same words may be applied but in a very different context.

Guardian[1]

G. B. CAIRD

THE NEW ENGLISH BIBLE was commissioned because the Authorized Version, for all the well-loved cadences of its majestic prose, does not convey to the modern reader what the original authors meant. Into the new version of the New Testament have gone the accumulated learning and wisdom of a century of scholarship, and what a magnificent and exciting achievement it is! The translators have aimed at accuracy and clarity and have achieved dignity and beauty as well.

In 350 years the English language has changed: 'We fetched a compass' (Acts 28[13], AV) does not mean what it once meant; 'prevent' (1 Thess 4[15]) does not mean 'forestall', nor does 'let' (2 Thess 2[7]) mean 'hinder', except at tennis. But archaism is only one reason for dissatisfaction with the Authorized Version. The best Greek text available in 1611 was seriously inaccurate. Since then older and more reliable manuscripts have been discovered. Among many textual changes, Mark 16[9-20] and John 7[53]-8[11] are printed as later additions, Luke 22[19-20] is relegated to a footnote, and 1 John 5[7] disappears without trace. Smaller changes may be no less important. 1 John 4[19] reads: 'We love because he first loved us', not 'We love *him*'.

From the Greek papyri we have gained more precise knowledge of the meaning of words. Jesus did not say of the prodigal that he 'gathered all together' (Lk 15[13], AV), but that he 'turned the whole of his share into cash' (*NEB*). Paul did not accuse the trouble-makers of Thessalonica of 'walking disorderly' (2 Thess 3[11], AV) but of 'idling their time away' (*NEB*). Even more important than such details is the discovery that New Testament Greek was far more colloquial than literary; and the new translation does justice to this throughout.

The New Testament authors wrote Greek with a Semitic flavour, and translators must allow for this. Paul did not say, 'He

[1] 14th March 1961, p. 8.

that is dead is freed from sin' (Rom 6[7], AV), but 'A dead man is no longer answerable for his sin' (*NEB*). It is not said of Noah that he 'condemned the world' (Heb 11[7], AV), but that he 'put the whole world in the wrong' (*NEB*).

I have so far found only one passage where the new translation seems to me less accurate that the Authorized Version—Acts 16[6], where an overscrupulous rendering of a past participle makes havoc of Paul's itinerary. (In New Testament Greek a past participle sometimes describes action subsequent to that of the main verb.)

Greek manuscripts had little or no punctuation, and in particular no quotation marks. How the narratives of Gospels and Acts come alive when printed with modern punctuation! What a difference a query can make to the sense! ('You knew that I reap where I have not sown, and gather where I have not scattered?' Mt 25[26].) There are passages in Paul's letters which take on new meaning when we recognize that he is debating, and that some things he says are not his own opinions but quotations from his opponent's argument.

We must not give the impression, however, that the *NEB* is a revision of the AV: it is a completely new version, based on a different principle of translation. Every schoolboy knows that there are two kinds of translation: one which substitutes an English word for each word of the original, leaving the sentence structure unchanged; and the harder way of thinking what the author meant and expressing that meaning in English idiom. The *NEB* belongs to the second category. Long sentences have been dissected to bring out the logical connexion of their clauses. Dead metaphors have been revitalized. Great theological utterances are made as lucid as their profundity allows.

The new approach raises new problems. It is one thing to modernize language, but what happens when it is the object or practice that is out of date? Here the translators have been rightly conservative. It is true that their thieves 'break in', instead of 'digging through'; but 'the winnowing shovel', 'the scroll', 'the woman's veil', 'the victor's garland' remain. They have not, however, kept the 'swaddling clothes', though here it is surely the custom, not the word, that is obsolete; and 'all wrapped up' is hardly a felicitous substitute. With money they are brilliantly successful—'a silverpiece', 'bags of gold' (for talents), 'a full day's wage', 'whose debt ran into millions'. The silver penny of 1611 could reasonably represent the denarius of the tribute money (Mk 12[15]), but I doubt whether even then it was a fair day's wage (Mt 20[16]). Certainly today 'A whole day's wage for a quart of flour' gives a better impression of famine than 'A measure of wheat for a penny' (Rev 6[6]).

Hebrew psychology distributes the personality throughout the body so that heart, veins, bowels, flesh and blood were conceived as having psychic functions. It is easy enough to make Paul call Onesimus 'a part of myself' instead of 'mine own bowels' (Phil 12). But what is to be done with a many-sided word like 'flesh', which so readily leads to the misapprehension that Paul located the seat of sin in the physical body? In John's Gospel, where the emphasis is on the reality of Christ's manhood, the *NEB* keeps 'flesh'; but in Paul's letters it becomes 'our lower nature' or 'our sinful nature'. Similarly 'blood' is kept in any context with eucharistic overtones, but elsewhere is rendered 'life's blood' or even 'sacrificial death'.

The use of many equivalents for a single term makes for clarity, but it involves some loss. Words have a meaning, but they also have associations on which much of their power depends. The biblical writers, like poets, used the evocative power of association. Thus when 'Gird up the loins of your mind' (1 Pet 1[13], AV) becomes 'You must therefore be like men stripped for action' (*NEB*), there is great gain in directness and intelligibility; but we miss the intended echo of the Passover rubric: 'Thus shall you eat it: your loins girded. . . .' The Fourth Gospel is the book in which association matters most, for woven into its texture are golden threads of meaning—'life', 'love', 'glory', 'send', 'abide', and others. In the place of 'abide', for example, the *NEB* uses ten different words and phrases, greatly improving the clarity of each context at the cost of the verbal link between them. As those who have laboured at it know best, translation is an impossible art: theological students must still learn Greek.

Religion in Life[1]

ERNEST C. COLWELL

... BEFORE TURNING[2] to an appraisal of the *New English Bible*, a glance is needed at one of the wilder paraphrases of the New Testament—the work of J. B. Phillips.[3] This is needed particularly by readers of Bruce, who speaks of its 'lasting acceptance' as 'one of the best [translations]—perhaps actually the best—for the ordinary reader'.[4] He defends Phillips from the charge of paraphrase by claiming that he gives us a 'meaning-for-meaning' translation. He does not point out Phillips's own confession of paraphrase in the preface of his first work, a confession unjustifiably repudiated in later work. The only Greek text ever mentioned by Phillips differs frequently and substantially from his version. In recent years I have checked twenty English translations as to the extent of their agreement with two Greek New Testaments—first the modern, scholarly Westcott and Hort's, and second with the late medieval corrupted New Testament commonly called the *Textus Receptus*.[5] The test was made in sixty-three passages throughout the Gospel of John, these sixty-three being all passages in which the Greek source is, usually, clearly discernible. In his 1958 edition Phillips says (on page x): 'I have worked directly in this translation from the best available Greek text.' As far as the Fourth Gospel is concerned, this statement is false. So far is his translation from being close to the best that it is closer to the worst available Greek text (the *Textus Receptus*) than is any other of the twenty in our test made from the Greek—except *KJ*. Whereas the RV, Phillips's standard, ranks fifth from the top in the list of twenty, Phillips ranks seventeenth with only

[1] Vol. XXXI, No. 2 (Spring 1962), pp. 294–302.

[2] From a consideration of F. F. Bruce, *The English Bible* (OUP, 1961), with which the reviewer had been dealing up to this point. (Ed.)

[3] *The New Testament in Modern English* (New York: Macmillan, 1958).

[4] *Op. cit.* p. 214. Contrast the sharp judgement of F. C. Grant that it belongs with 'translations' which are really paraphrases. *Translating the Bible* (Greenwich: Seabury Press, 1961), p. 101.

[5] See E. C. Colwell, *What Is the Best New Testament?* (Chicago: University of Chicago Press, 1952), pp. 85–104.

thirty-five agreements with Westcott and Hort against *Textus Receptus* out of the sixty-three.

Accuracy is achieved not only through the use of an accurate source but also through accurate methods of translating. Phillips's method of translating is not characterized by accuracy.[6] Even Bruce withdraws his approval from rendering 'In the beginning was the Word' (Jn 1[1]) by 'At the beginning God expressed himself'. Mr Phillips's own doctrines and tastes enter the New Testament through his translation. He prefers 'love' to 'grace' (Jn 1[17]). He prefers an understanding of human nature to a superhuman knowledge of what a man was thinking (2[25]). He dislikes rudeness or abruptness to women; so he adds 'please' to the request for a drink (4[7]) and omits 'Woman' in Jesus's brusque repudiation of his mother's directions in 2[4], smoothing it out to: 'Is that your concern, or mine?' The 'please' is an example of the translator's good manners; it is impossible on the lips of the Jesus of the Fourth Gospel who takes directions from no one and makes no real request of anyone except God. He achieves a low conversational style by the addition of fillers: 'it is true', 'of course', 'you know' (1[18, 27, 33]; 4[25, 33]; 5[10], etc.).

In the early chapters of John the very worst example of perversion lies in Phillips's insertion of the doctrine of the incarnation in his own terms. This is to be seen in the following list of passages, where the word 'Man' with a capital M was inserted in the 1952 translation of the Gospels (in only one of them does the Greek contain a word for 'man' (1[30]), but even in that passage the word 'man' is the colourless $\dot{a}\nu\dot{\eta}\rho$ and not $\ddot{a}\nu\theta\rho\omega\pi\text{os}$): 1[26, 30], 1[33, 45], 4[42]. This last passage is so inexcusable that it should be quoted: 'We know now that this is really ("must be", 1958) the Man ("man", 1958) who will save the world' for 'We know that this is, indeed, the saviour of the world' (*RSV*). The insertion of the word 'man' in all these passages, even where it is kept with a small letter in 1958, is one of the clearest instances to be found in all the history of modern translation of the imposition upon the Gospel text of the translator's own ideas. Anyone who interpreted the Fourth Gospel on the basis of Phillips's translation would be led far astray by Mr Phillips's contribution to the text of the Gospel in these passages. In general, especially in Phillips's first work, the reader will find these paraphrases stimulating and therefore

[6] For my own convenience I choose my examples from the Gospel of John.

valuable—but not dependable for serious study of the New Testament.

Bruce announces but does not discuss the most important recent English translation: the *New English Bible*. The boldest thing about the *New English Bible* is that it is a new translation, not a revision of older translations. In this new translation, style is king, and whenever accuracy or clarity interfere with style, they are sacrificed.

The translation clearly reveals that certain specific concepts of good English prose style were ruthlessly imposed upon the work of the translators. Among these canons of good style were (1) short sentences, (2) no repetition, (3) simple sentences rather than complex, (4) all biblicisms such as 'it came to pass' to be omitted, (5) freshly contemporary language.

These 'rules' I derived from a sampling of the translation. Yet the most notable of them are strikingly reminiscent of Jowett's principles stated in his Preface to his *Plato*.[7] Unfortunately, the translators were not Jowett; they were committees. The great translations that achieved style were the work of one man (e.g. Tyndale, Moffatt, Goodspeed), not of committees. It may be argued that the *King James* disproves this. But does it? Students of this revision of the New Testament admit that ninety per cent of it is the work of Tyndale. Is it possible that the achievement of the *King James* style is, in the New Testament, essentially the achievement of one man named Tyndale? . . .[8]

No essay on the translation of the New Testament can avoid a discussion of the Greek text used as source. . . . The *King James* revisers used the corrupt, late-medieval Greek text—the only text available to them. Moffatt unfortunately translated from Soden's Greek text—a text now universally repudiated by scholars. Goodspeed used Westcott and Hort's text—one of the fine flowers of nineteenth-century textual criticism, still unreplaced by any different type of text. The *RSV* committee used various texts and drew on variant readings from the margins. Their choice of a Greek reading was not determined by external (that is, manuscript) evidence, but by the internal evidence of readings. Their criteria were: (*a*) Which reading best fits the context? and (*b*) Which

---

[7] See F. C. Grant's interesting discussion of the relevance of Jowett's principles to biblical translations in *Translating the Bible*, pp. 130–41.
[8] *Ibid.*, pp. 63–5.

reading if taken to be original best explains the origin of the other readings ? Their text is, therefore, eclectic and unidentifiable. But with the list of sixty-three readings in John used above for Phillips, we can place *RSV* between Westcott and Hort and the corrupt medieval text that lies behind *King James*. In that list, *RSV* agrees with Westcott and Hort fifty-four times, with the other extreme eight times, and once with something else. Thus its Greek text approximates the modern scholarly editions.

The *New English Bible* translators employed the methods used by the *RSV*. They chose individual readings rather than a single edition of the Greek New Testament, and Professor Dodd told me that they relied on the two criteria used by the *RSV*. This leads one to expect the same kind of basic Greek text.

But the *NEB* is much weaker than *RSV* in its treatment of the Greek text, at least in John. In the list of sixty-three readings it agrees with Westcott and Hort only forty times, with the *Textus Receptus* fifteen times, and with something else eight times.[9] *NEB* stands fifteenth in the list of twenty translations, followed only by Confraternity, Phillips, Knox, Challoner, and *King James*. Only Phillips of the sixteen modern translations from the Greek is further from Westcott and Hort than the *New English Bible*.

How is this difference between *RSV* and *NEB* to be explained ? A part of the difference lies in the greater freedom of the new translation as contrasted with the limitations of a revision. But more important is the nature of the *American Standard Version*, the base for the *RSV*. That base was extreme in its devotion to 'faithfulness' and 'accuracy', and that faithfulness was to a text very close to that of Westcott and Hort. But a translation starting from scratch, choosing individual readings as such without the balancing weight of an appraisal of individual manuscripts or groups of manuscripts, can go in any direction and, most easily, downhill. Hence the superiority of *RSV* in relation to the text of the Greek New Testament.

The marginal citation of manuscript evidence in *NEB* is disappointing. After all, this is a *new* translation. Was it too much to expect that it might avoid blurring the evidence of various witnesses into one label: 'Some witnesses read' ? Indications of the relative number and age of these witnesses are possible without

---

[9] It is possible that the paraphrastic nature of the translation may explain these eight passages, but they are not in agreement with Westcott and Hort.

great distortion, and might at the least prevent the inevitable misunderstanding caused by the present system. In Matthew 27^{16-17} the text of *NEB* twice refers to Bar-Abbas as 'Jesus Bar-Abbas', and the margin says (as usual), '*Some witnesses omit Jesus*'. The implication for the non-specialist reader is that 'most witnesses' and/or 'the earliest witnesses' read 'Jesus Bar-Abbas' and 'some witnesses', i.e. few or late or unimportant, read 'Bar-Abbas'. The facts are that only nine witnesses, only one of them early or externally significant, read: 'Jesus Bar-Abbas.'[10]

Let us say of the *New English Bible*, in conclusion, that it is a brave thing to make a new translation. It is a new translation which, at times, achieves a fine prose style, but it is uneven in quality, inconsistent in execution, and, as one of its translators said in a recent lecture, to be used for the stimulation of Bible-study, since it is too free to be used itself for serious study.

[10] But see further p. 51.

Concordia Theological Monthly[1]

FREDERICK W. DANKER

THE APPEARANCE of *The New English Bible: New Testament* (*NEB*)[2] may mark one of the most significant English religious publications since the Holy Scriptures first went to Press. This work is not a retouching of old masters but wears with proud distinction and integrity the title 'New'. Because it communicates in timely idiom and yet with timeless phrase it merits classification with the choicest products of *English* Literary art. The lavish scholarly resources that entered into its production are unparalleled in history. To enter into critical judgement with a work of such magnitude is no mean task. The best that we can hope to do is communicate something of the genius of this notable publication, to express appreciation, and to pinpoint areas for further consideration.

Since there is nothing quite like this publication in the history of the translation of the sacred Scriptures into English, we are at a loss to find something to which we can 'liken it'. Any previous translations or revision will seem less brilliant by comparison. Yet some kind of comparative analysis is necessary to convey even a small appreciation of the critical excellences and deficiencies of this new venture. Since the *Revised Standard Version* (*RSV*) will be the nearest competitor of this translation we shall in the course of this study make frequent references to that version.[3] The reader must keep in mind, however, that the committee responsible for *RSV* was carrying out instructions to retain as much as possible of the flavour of the *King James Version* and its descendants and did

[1] Vol. XXXII, No. 6 (June 1961), pp. 334–47.

[2] The author is grateful to the publishers of the St Louis *Globe-Democrat* for permission to incorporate material published under his name, 19th March 1961, pp. 4f.

[3] Unless otherwise specified, reference is made to the edition of the complete Bible published in 1952. For a critique of the version see my *Multipurpose Tools for Bible Study* (St Louis, 1960), pp. 180–4. The *Reference Edition with Concise Concordance* (New York, 1959) introduced significant alterations and corrections and is referred to in the footnotes as *RSV*[(3)].

not enjoy the same freedom that the translators of *NEB* display. Certain excellences therefore of the latter translation must be recognized without disparagement to those responsible for *RSV*. Ultimately it is the reading public who will decide which version is to be preferred for either private or public use. To help provide a portion of the data for the forming of sound judgement is the burden of this study.

IDIOMATIC ENGLISH

The first test of a work which claims to be a new translation is whether it communicates in contemporary terms without erasing to the point of illegibility the historical gap. Felicitous expressions meet one everywhere in astounding prodigality. There is the rasp of desert sand in words like these, 'No bullying; no blackmail; make do with your pay!' (Lk 3¹⁴), that captures the man who dared to take the path to greatness through the obscure way. The social game of petty character sniping comes to a halt at words like these:

Why do you look at the speck of sawdust in your brother's eye, with never a thought for the great plank in your own? How can you say to your brother, 'My dear brother, let me take the speck out of your eye', when you are blind to the plank in your own? You hypocrite! First take the plank out of your own eye, and then you will see clearly to take the speck out of your brother's.

RSV landlubbers caught none of the spray in Matthew 14²⁴. It takes a seafaring people to picture the disciples 'battling with a head-wind and a rough sea'. Another meteorological phenomenon is neatly documented in Luke 12⁵⁵: 'And when the wind is from the south, you say, "There will be a heat-wave," and there is.' Of the conniving Pharisees it is said parenthetically that '(Their aim was to frame a charge against him).' Contrast this with *RSV*'s less virile 'so that they might accuse Him' (Mat 12¹⁰). Once Paul proudly trotted out the family album and held up his coat-of-arms, only casually to cancel out the glittering lineage of 'a Hebrew born and bred' (Phil 3⁵), with the line: 'But all such assets I have written off because of Christ' (Phil 3⁷). To underscore his meaning he counts it 'so much garbage' (Phil 3⁸). *RSV* perfumed the stench with a squeamish "I . . . count them as refuse". In Matthew 18²⁴, *NEB* spares us the use of a monetary slide rule; the unforgiving rascal's debt, we are told, 'ran into millions'. And in Philippians 2²⁰ Paul characterizes Timothy—'There is no one else here who sees things as I do'. These are but a few examples picked at random. Every page sparkles with the brilliance of idiomatic clarity. But does the translation purchase such gems of facile and contemporaneous expression at the expense of integrity and accuracy?

JOTS AND TITTLES

The scholars responsible for this translation profess that they have endeavoured to avoid slipshod work. The results bear out the validity of their claim. In meticulous attention to the text, *NEB* outshines *RSV*. . . .

LEXICOGRAPHY

In John 7⁸, *RSV* overlooks the force of ταύτην;[4] *NEB* correctly renders; 'I am not going up to *this* festival.' On the other hand, in Matthew 21⁵, we find *RSV* more accurately reflecting Matthew's understanding of the prophecy from Zechariah. *NEB* fails to translate the second significant καί.

The precision of Paul's references to homosexual perversions in 1 Corinthians 6⁹ is not maintained by *NEB*'s paraphrase, 'Homosexual perversion', although this rendering is more accurate than *RSV*'s paraphrase: 'Homosexuals.' It is the perverted act that Paul decries, not a physical or psychological condition. On the other hand, the original specifies males, specifically 'catamites' and 'sodomites', to which *RSV* makes allusions in a marginal note— 'Two Greek words are rendered by this expression'. *NEB* contains no note on the passage.

The phrase, 'vessels which were objects of retribution due for destruction' (*NEB*, Rom 9²²), stresses the historical perspective suggested by the context more than *RSV*'s 'made for destruction'. 'I have not come to invite virtuous people, but to call sinners to repentance' (Lk 5³²) expresses precisely the point made in Luke's Gospel. Jesus recognizes valid legal attainments, but He wants Israel's religious élite to share the experience of God's love.

NEB manages to combine idiomatic grace with literal conversion of the metaphor in Jude 4, rendering: 'the very men whom *Scripture* long ago *marked* down'. Contrast this with *RSV*'s 'some who long ago were designated'.

---

⁴ Corrected in *RSV*⁽³⁾.

'Enforced justice' (*RSV*, Heb 11³³) expresses an ambiguity not found in the original; *NEB*'s 'established justice' fits philological requirements. Similarly in Hebrews 12¹⁷, *NEB* exactly expresses Esau's tragic circumstance, 'he found no way open for second thoughts'; *RSV* ('found no chance to repent') prompts a sympathetic tear for Esau but suggests to the heedless reader a misrepresentation of the writer's thoughts.

NEB handles well the phrase, πρώτην πίστιν ἠθέτησαν (1 Tim 5¹²), condemned 'for breaking their *troth* with Him'. *RSV* renders 'first pledge'.

RSV claims to be able to classify with some precision Jonah's marvellous aquatic hotel, but *NEB*, as does the original, leaves the zoological slot undetermined and advisedly renders 'sea-monster' (Mt 12⁴⁰). *RSV*'s 'weeds' (Mt 13²⁵) might also be pulled out in favour of the more accurate 'darnel' of *NEB*. What is the force of ἀπό in Hebrews 13²⁴? *NEB* preserves what is now an ambiguity with the happy rendering: 'Greetings to you from our Italian friends.' *RSV* more confidently: 'Those who come from Italy send you greetings.'

Luke's entire prologue reads more fluently and precisely in *NEB* than in *RSV*. *NEB*'s rendering 'as one who has gone over the whole course of events in detail' (1³) is preferable philologically as well as stylistically to *RSV*'s 'having followed all things closely for some time past'.[5]

There appears in James 2⁴ a refractory διεκρίθητε. The British render: 'do you not see that you are *inconsistent* and judge by false standards?' *RSV* offers the nondescript, 'have you not made distinctions among yourselves . . . ?'

John 1⁵ with its use of the word καταλαμβάνω drives translators to despair. *RSV* render: 'the darkness has not *overcome it*' (i.e. the Light). *NEB* interprets 'has never *quenched* it'. Neither version alerts the reader to the ambivalence, involving the thoughts both of hostility and mental apprehension. A problem passage like this (and it is but one of many) should of course remind the student that no translation, not even such masterful works as *RSV* and *NEB*, can relieve him of the necessity of learning Greek and maintaining its mastery. (For a similar problem see John 3³⁶, ἀπειθέω).[6]

---

[5] See J. M. Creed, *The Gospel According to St Luke, ad loc.*, in the passage.

[6] Corrected in *RSV*⁽³⁾.

SYNONYMS

The translators responsible for both *RSV* and *NEB* wisely refrained from attempting to render uniformly a Greek word with a single English equivalent. In this respect they emulated their predecessors responsible for the *KJV* who in guileless accents of destiny defended their use of synonyms on the ground that if they dealt unequally with a number of good English words some of them might be banished for ever. They are equally aware that synonyms in one language may be adequately expressed by a single word in another language. However, on some passages there may be legitimate debate, and it is the translator's obligation to provide his reader with the data, as long as he does not thereby obscure his author's intent. *NEB* encourages confidence in the reader by distinguishing carefully the two verbs, κηρύσσω and εὐαγγελίζω in 1 Peter 3[19] and 4[6] respectively. Jesus 'made his *proclamation* to the imprisoned spirits' (3[19]), and the Gospel was '*preached* to those who are dead' (4[6]). *RSV* closes the debate by rendering both terms with 'preach'. Similarly in Luke 1[42 and 45] *NEB* reveals that two different Greek words are used; *RSV* renders both with 'Blessed'.

TAKE YOUR CHOICE

In many cases a word may be understood differently in the same passage. Thus *NEB* (like *RSV*) reads 'elemental spirits of the universe' in Galatians 4[3] (see also verse 9; Col 2[8, 20]) with the note '*or*, the elements of the natural world, *or* elementary ideas belonging to this world'. Again, in 1 Corinthians 7[36] an alternative 'virgin daughter' is noted in the margin. *RSV* also noted alternative renderings in passages containing ambiguities of this nature, but neither version follows a consistent pattern. Thus for the two passages just mentioned *RSV* includes no marginal notes. On the other hand the American version offers more data than *NEB* in a section like 1 Corinthians 1–6 (see especially 4[17] and 5[11]).

GRAMMATICAL PROBLEMS

The translator's precision will betray itself especially in the handling of a highly inflected language. Although the Koine of the New Testament does not display the fine classical distinctions, yet tenses and voices are not used indiscriminately. Certainly *RSV*'s grammatical sensitivity falters in the rendering, 'all were baptized into Moses' (1 Cor 10²). The form is middle and the British reproduce it faithfully: 'they all received baptism'. Precision is important here because Paul's point is that the Israelites accepted Moses' leadership by getting themselves baptized, as it were, in the crossing of the Red Sea. *NEB* preserves an active voice in Ephesians 5²⁷. *RSV* reads: 'that the church might be presented before Him.'⁷ *NEB* drops the words $\mu\eta\delta\grave{\epsilon}\nu$ $\delta\iota\alpha\kappa\rho\acute{\iota}\nu\alpha\nu\tau\alpha$ (Acts 11¹²) into the margin, but offers a more accurate translation ('making no distinctions') than *RSV*, which treated the active as a middle: 'without hesitation.'⁸

RSV's rendering of Mark 9³⁸ would suggest that the disciples were proud of the fact that they had successfully restrained a non-union exorcist—'we forbade him'. *NEB* captures the true situation described in the imperfect $\grave{\epsilon}\kappa\omega\lambda\acute{\nu}o\mu\epsilon\nu$, 'we tried to stop him'. The Gadarenes 'took to their heels', says *NEB* (Mt 8³³), translating the aorist $\grave{\epsilon}\phi\nu\gamma o\nu$; *RSV*: 'The herdsmen fled.' In Matthew 21³⁸ the rebel tenants exclaim in *RSV*: 'This is the heir; come, let us kill him and have his inheritance.' *NEB* again displays a superior grammatical awareness of the aorist $\sigma\chi\hat{\omega}\mu\epsilon\nu$: 'Let us kill him, and *get* his inheritance.' Mark 1³⁶ reads in *RSV*: 'And Simon and those who were with him *followed* Him.' *NEB* notes the aorist: 'But Simon and his companions *searched* Him *out*.' That is translating. Unlike *RSV*, *NEB* displays awareness of the perfect tense in John 11²⁷ and renders: 'I now believe.' And in John 20³¹ the present tense of $\pi\iota\sigma\tau\epsilon\acute{\nu}\omega$ is caught up in the wording: 'Those here written have been recorded in order that you may hold the faith.' Only occasionally does *NEB* miss the force of a verb, as in Mark 1¹², where *RSV* is to be preferred.

Inflected pronouns are occasionally too supple for a precise translation into a language of meagre inflections. *RSV* is content with a note alerting to the change of you from plural to singular in the original of Luke 22³¹⁻². *NEB* lives up to its claim not to be slipshod and deftly renders: 'Simon, Simon, take heed: Satan has been given leave to sift all of you like wheat; but for you I have prayed that your faith may not fail.' That is quality work. Nor is this an isolated occurrence. A parallel phenomenon occurs in John 1⁵⁰⁻¹. Here *RSV* does not even bother with a marginal note; *NEB* again comes through with a clear reproduction of pronominal distinctions in the original.

⁷ Corrected in *RSV*⁽³⁾.   ⁸ Corrected in *RSV*⁽³⁾.

SEMITISM

RSV was apparently embarrassed by the Semitism in Heb 6[14]. The *NEB* has naturalized this alien tautology; 'I vow that I will bless you abundantly and multiply your descendants.' With similar grace *NEB* renders a pleonasm in Colossians 2[1] with the phrase: 'the Laodiceans and all who have never set eyes on me.'

SYNTAX

Syntactical relations often require an especially sensitive comprehension, bred by long acquaintance with the language. Several logical interpretations may be offered for a series of words, but only one, except when we are dealing with a slipshod writer, can ordinarily be correct.

John 20[19 and 20] contains a sample of the kind of see-saw material that can plague the interpreter. In this case *NEB* has unmistakably sensed the intimate connection between the peace announced by Jesus and the price our Lord paid for it. '"Peace be with you!" he said, and then showed them His hands and His side.' *RSV* partially breaks the link.

Does ὁ ὤν in Romans 9[5] go with θεός, which follows, or with ὁ Χριστός, which precedes? To charge either *RSV* or *NEB* with wilful refusal to support the doctrine of the deity of Jesus Christ because they both interpret the latter half of the verse as an independent doxology would be indicative not only of uncharitable judgement but also of profound ignorance of the entire subject of Pauline theology, not to speak of such passages as Titus 2[13] and 2 Peter 1[1], where the deity of Jesus Christ is strongly affirmed in contrast with the interpretation of the *King James Version*. Both versions include the minority reports of their committees, so that the reader has access to the data on essential points like this.

In some cases the Greekless reader can only recognize the existence of a syntactical problem by comparing the two versions. Thus *RSV* reads: 'When we cry "Abba! Father!" it is the Spirit Himself bearing witness with our spirit that we are children of God' (Rom 8[15-16]). *NEB* reads: 'The Spirit you have received is ...a Spirit that makes us sons, enabling us to cry "Abba! Father!"' In that cry the Spirit of God joins with our spirit in testifying that we are God's children. In either case the meaning is clear and it may be that Paul knew what he wanted to say, but on reading it over also recognized the ambiguity. But he might have said to himself: 'Either way. To have the Spirit is to be a son. To be a son means to cry Abba! Father!' Neither version includes a marginal note on the passage. . . .

PARAPHRASE OR LITERAL TRANSLATION

In their introductory remarks the translators of *NEB* frankly acknowledge that they do not hesitate to resort to paraphrase when the intent of the original can be expressed adequately in no other way. They will be criticized for this by those who forget that *KJV* and *RSV* frequently do the same thing. A notable instance of paraphrase in *RSV* is 1 Corinthians 16^{12}, where God is made responsible for Apollos's failure to visit Corinth. The word θεός does not occur in the text. *NEB* makes Apollos responsible for the decision, with a marginal note acknowledging the alternative adopted by *RSV*. The margin in *RSV* notes the paraphrase which *NEB* adopts in the text.

In Hebrews 2^8 *RSV* utilizes the interpretive paraphrase, 'in subjection to *man*'.[9] This rendering brings out the point made by the author of Hebrews that the words of Psalm 8$^{5-7}$, LXX, cannot really be understood apart from Jesus Christ. The psalm says all things have been subjected to man, but this is not really true, says the writer of Hebrews, if ordinary men only are kept in mind (Heb 2^8). But there is a man to whom these words do apply, *Jesus*, who was made a little lower than angels, but now has all things under His control. *NEB* is more literal but not so helpful to the reader as on other occasions. . . .

The causal connection between forgiveness and love's response is securely caught in the story of the grateful sinner, 'her great love proves that her many sins have been forgiven' (*NEB*, Lk 7^{47}; *RSV* not so clearly).

1 Timothy 3^2 is a passage that not only tests the skill of the private interpreter but the integrity of a committee dedicated to an honest reproduction of the text. Once again the British toss it off with aplomb. Not only is the historical evolution of ecclesiastical offices recognized ('Our leader, therefore, or bishop,' begins the verse) but the delicate matter of the 'bishop's' marital conduct is tactfully disposed of in the phrase, 'faithful to his one wife'. Polygamy is hardly condemned here by the writer, otherwise

[9] *RSV*$^{(3)}$ reads, 'in subjection to him'.

polyandry must be inferred in 5[9]. 'Married only once' (*RSV*, with a note to the effect that the Greek reads 'the husband of one wife') is not an impossible rendering, but the context emphasizes present attitudes and skills.[10] Yet these minority reports are there in *NEB*'s margin.

NEB sounds the explicit eschatological note in Matthew 5[6] with the words: 'How blest are those who hunger and thirst to see right prevail.' It is the Messianic hope for deliverance, the end-time display of God's 'righteousness' or 'deliverance', prophesied by Isaiah (46[13], LXX), which is described here. God's people need not wait any longer. In the person of Jesus 'they shall be satisfied'.

Did John the Baptist appear 'dressed in silks and satins?' asks Jesus (*NEB*, Lk 7[25]). Contrast this with *RSV*'s mothballed 'raiment'. What was the ship 'Twin Brothers' (*RSV*, Acts 28[11])? *NEB* tells us: 'the *Castor and Pollux*.' And who will fail to feel the bite of 'tooth and nail' in Galatians 5[15]?

Readers with a background in the Old Testament will readily associate God with the 'wrath' mentioned in Romans 12[19], but for him who reads on the run, *NEB* thoughtfully amplifies: 'leave a place for divine retribution.'

Contrast *NEB*'s pungent expansion of κατατομήν in Philippians 3[2], 'Beware of those who insist on mutilation—"circumcision" I will not call it', with *RSV*'s pedestrian paraphrase: 'look out for those who mutilate the flesh.' Paul is blunt, too blunt sometimes for modern ears. It is a display of the loftiest art to communicate his sense without offence—*NEB* succeeds. And who can fail to understand Paul when he says in the same letter; 'I have been very thoroughly initiated into the human lot with all its ups and downs' (*NEB*, Phil 4[12]).

The grumbling of disappointment is expressed in no uncertain terms in John 6[60]: 'This is more than we can stomach! Why listen to such words?' (*NEB*). Contrast this with *RSV*'s 'This is a hard saying; who can listen to it?' More literal indeed, but will the rank-and-file digest it?

In Romans 2[28-9] *RSV* added the word 'real' or 'true' several times. *NEB* follows this lead and expresses with an additional word what the Greek can express by word position. The original, one might say, is being 'fortified' to protect the text against loss of

---

[10] *RSV*[(3)] reads 'husband of one wife', (1 Tim 3[2], [12], Titus 1[6]), 'wife of one husband' (1 Tim 5[9]).

meaning in translation. Luther did this in his notable, to some notorious, rendering of Romans 3[28].

'Friend, do what you are here to do' is *NEB*'s paraphrase of a difficult ellipse in Matthew 26[50]. One can scarcely imagine a more precise rendering to contrast Jesus's regal bearing and Judas's cheap hypocrisy. Never mind the formalities, says Jesus. Take care of the business you're here for!

What is the meaning of 1 Corinthians 9[24]? From *RSV* one might infer that since only one can win the prize, the Christian must be sure to be the first one to break the tape. *NEB* more intelligibly suggests that Paul does not race dry his own metaphor: 'Like them, run to win!' That is a real demonstration of the translator's art, not to speak of careful scholarship.

It is clear that both versions indulge in frequent paraphrase. The reader will be able to discover for himself that *NEB* incidence is higher than *RSV*'s. This is to be expected, since *NEB* aims at a completely new translation rather than a revision of previous versions. On the other hand we regret that *NEB* has not made a few more expansions of the text in the interests of clarity. Instead of imitating *RSV*'s obscure 'spirits of just men made perfect' (Heb 12[23]),[11] *NEB* might have provided some hint that moral perfection is not the concern here, but rather that these are people who now enjoy the fulfilment of their hopes.

THEOLOGY

As far as we can observe, *NEB* grinds no theological axes. Scrupulous regard for the text is a prime consideration. Hence the un-Pauline theology in *RSV*'s rendering of Romans 3[30], 'justify . . . the uncircumcised because of their faith' is not supported by *NEB*, which correctly renders: '*through* their faith.'[12] The phrase 'through his blood' is omitted by the British (as in *RSV*) in the translation of Colossians 1[14], and for textual-critical reasons, but the same statement will be found in Ephesians 1[7].

RSV's 'destined' (1 Pet 2[8]), suggests to the untrained reader a specific theological concept not implied in the Greek. The original is less technical, and *NEB* happily renders; 'Such was their appointed lot.' Again, in Titus 3[5], *NEB* properly accents the Holy

---

[11] *NEB* reads: 'spirits of good men made perfect.'
[12] This is also the corrected reading of *RSV*[(3)].

Spirit as source of the renewal mentioned; *RSV* emphasizes the qualitative aspect: 'renewal in the Holy Spirit.'

NEB is less ambiguous than *RSV* in the translation of Revelation 20$^{4-5}$. The meaning turns on the force of ἔζησαν in both verses. *NEB* renders 'came to life again' in verse 4, but the rendering 'though the rest of the dead did not come to life' in verse 5 clearly shows that the British committee does not wish its adverbial additive 'again' to be understood in the sense of a double resurrection. *RSV*, which employs 'again' in both cases, may offer undesigned comfort to distorters of Johannine eschatology.[13]

How does faith show itself? *NEB* offers for James 2^{22} not only an idiomatically expressive rendering but also one that is philologically precise: 'by these actions the integrity of his faith was fully proved.' This is much superior to *RSV*'s literal but equivocal 'faith was completed by works'.

According to *RSV*, Hebrews 4^{15} views our Lord's sinlessness quantitatively, with accent on the overt act; *NEB* renders literally; 'without sin.' C. H. Dodd's work on 'realized eschatology' surfaces in the rendering of Mark 9^1.

NEB's treatment of ἐκκλησία will undoubtedly arouse much comment and therefore calls for more extensive discussion. Like *KJV* and *RSV*, the British translators do not hesitate to use different terms to express the meaning of this word. *KJV*, however, limited its deviation from the rendering 'church' to Acts 19$^{32, 39, 41}$, which called for the less technical English expression, 'assembly'. *RSV*, in addition to the passages in Acts 19, introduces this rendering in Hebrews 12^{23}, echoing its normal reproduction of *qāhāl* in the Old Testament. In Acts 7^{38} and Hebrews 2^{12}, *RSV* uses 'congregation', in reference to the Israel of the Old Testament; the word 'church' is reserved by *RSV* exclusively for definition of the *Christian* believers (74 times). The 'studied avoidance of uniformity' in *NEB*'s rendering of ἐκκλησία produces 'church', 'assembly', 'congregation', 'community', and 'meeting', with certain discernible patterns. 'Church' is the normal rendering when notice is taken simply of God's redeemed people, without reference to geography (Mt 16^{18}; Acts 5^{11}, 8^3; 9^{31}; 1 Cor 10^{32}, 11^{22}, 15^9; Gal 1^{13}; Eph 1^{22}; 1 Tim 3^{15}). Inconsistencies in this respect are references to the 'church' in Jerusalem (Acts 11^{22}) and in the cities of Asia Minor (Rev 1–3), whereas the

---

[13] *RSV*$^{(3)}$ omits the word 'again'.

Christians in Antioch (Acts 11²⁶) and in Corinth (1 Cor 1²) form a 'congregation', the term ordinarily used by *NEB* to define a specific group of Christians in a given locality (see e.g. Mt 18¹⁷; Acts 14²³, 20¹⁸; Rom 16¹). When the plural ἐκκλησίαι occurs, *NEB*, with the exception of Revelation 22¹⁶, renders 'congregations'. Where mutual edification is implied with emphasis on the reciprocal sharing of the Spirit's gifts, *NEB* felicitously renders 'community' (1 Cor 12²⁸ and 14⁴), the context clearly indicating the type of community that is meant; however, the use of 'church' (14¹²) in the same context comes as a surprise. *NEB* renders ἐκκλησία with 'assembly' in Acts 19³², ³⁹, ⁴¹, Hebrews 2¹², 12²³. The rendering 'meeting' appears twice (1 Cor 14²⁸, ³⁴). Occasionally the original expression is paraphrased, as in Acts 7³⁸; 'when they were assembled there in the desert'; in 2 Corinthians 8¹⁹ 'they' refers back to the previous verse.

On the whole we are convinced that the doctrine of the church finds more expressive enunciation in *NEB* than in either *KJV* or *RSV*. The pattern of consistency traced by the translators in dealing with a term that refracts in so many hues suggests no low aim.

TEXT

In the main *NEB*, like *RSV*, reflects the Westcott–Hort tradition and the student will note but few departures from the text in Nestle, although *NEB*, in line with recent trends in textual criticism, is inclined to be a little freer in these departures than *RSV*. One might, however, have anticipated that the British translators would have profited from the discomfiture of the sponsors of *RSV*, who were quick to change 'some' and 'many ancient authorities' (*RSV*, 1946) to simply 'other ancient authorities' (1952). *NEB*'s almost uniform 'some witnesses' is something less than informative.

NEB's rendering of Matthew 27¹⁶, ¹⁸ is an indication of the increased respect enjoyed by manuscripts other than *Vaticanus* and *Sinaiticus* and by the versions. The translators read 'Jesus Bar-Abbas'. This reading is to be preferred, not only because its absence in many manuscripts is quite probably an intentional scribal omission designed to maintain our Lord's dignity but also because it clarifies Pilate's description of Jesus as the one called Messiah. The governor has two men before him. Which one do they want? The marginal note 'Some witnesses omit Jesus' might suggest that the preponderant manuscript evidence supports the translation, whereas Nestle records only Θλ sy^{s-pal} Or; h^r in its apparatus. In contrast, at Luke 1^{46}, NEB observes that 'the majority of ancient witnesses' read 'Mary'.

In John 19^{29}, NEB, on the authority of a single witness, 476 *prima manu*, reads 'javelin' in place of RSV's hyssop. The reading ὑσσώπῳ is probably a very early corruption. Not only does it fail to make sense in the passage (the plant would hardly be suitable for raising up a wet sponge) but it looks like a scribe's intentional conformation of the events with Exodus 12^{22}.[14]

It is not clear what the British translators have done with Mark 1^{41}. They apparently prefer the reading ὀργισθείς, but interpret our Lord's anger as 'warm indignation', probably in the light of the context. On the other hand, we may have here a case of conflate 'mugwumping', despite the marginal notations, the mercy of the rejected reading combining with the anger of the preferred reading. Yet in view of the assurances in the introduction that the translators do not 'remain on the fence', we must in charity conclude that we deal here with a genuine paraphrase. *Remis velisque!* once again we say to owners of a Greek Testament.

The only conjectural emendation of the text I have located to date in NEB is in Matthew 2^6; 'Bethlehem in the land of Judah.' The Greek reads καὶ σὺ βηθλεέμ, γῆ 'Ιούδα. It may be, however, that the grammatical connections in the original are loose. NEB does not adopt RSV's conjectural omission of Κύριος in Jude 5.

Most of the significant variations are noted by both versions in the margins, with considerable variation in treatment. But a future edition of NEB ought to strive for greater consistency. The washing of 'beds' (Mark 7^4) is noted by RSV in the margin, but NEB fails to alert the reader to a reading which, though it is probably not original, nevertheless enjoys widespread support. Like RSV, NEB fails to note the fact that Matthew 9^{13} has omitted the words 'to repentance', read by the *Textus Receptus*.

CRITICAL SENSIBILITIES

NEB, like RSV, displays the broad knowledge that only intimate acquaintance with the problems of biblical research can promote,

[14] C. K. Barrett, *The Gospel According to St John* (New York, 1957), p. 460, defends the traditional reading.

and it has tried to bridge the gap between the study and the pew. But the customary reluctance of British scholars as a whole to reflect the findings of Continental form historians reveals itself in passages where Κύριος, when used as a vocative, is rendered 'Sir!' thus obscuring the theological perspective from which the Gospels are written. In this respect *RSV*'s readings are to be preferred, unless in a future edition the British note the alternate expression in the margin, or in the introduction alert the reader to their procedure in this and other matters. Moreover, as in the case of pronominal distinctions, *NEB* founders on the reefs of inconsistency. Are we to assume that the leper who says 'Sir' (Mat 8[6]) displayed less appreciation of Jesus's person than the cowardly disciples who say 'Lord' a few verses later (8[25]; see also 8[21])? In Matthew 15[21-8] the whole point is lost in the 'Sir' (15[22, 25, 27]). The children, the 'lords' of their dogs, take care of their charges; Jesus, the Lord, must do the same for His dependants. That was the dimension of the woman's faith, as Matthew relates it.

The nineteenth-century quest for the historical Jesus is evident in both versions; 'Truly this man was a son of God' (Mk 15[39]; cf. Mt 27[54]),[15] and the omission in *NEB* of the second καί displays a failure to note Matthew's concern to show express fulfilment of Zech 9[9] (Mt 21[5]).

PUNCTUATION

The careful Bible student must observe the telling use of punctuation marks in both versions. John 8[26] reads in *NEB*: 'I have much to say about you—and in judgement.' In a marginal note *NEB* observes that Jesus might well have asked the centurion: 'Am I to come and cure' your son? (Mt 8[7]). *RSV* lacks this information notation. Contrary to *RSV*'s understanding of the passage, *NEB* cites John 3[16] as part of the conversation ascribed to Jesus, but like *RSV* views John 3[31-6] as the evangelist's editorial comment. In connection with both passages *RSV* notes alternative punctuation; *NEB* does not indicate the option. Both versions usually signal phrasing from the Old Testament and quotations from secular authors by the use of quotation marks as in Ephesians 6[2] and 1 Corinthians 15[33]. In the absence of a specific rubric in the text, *NEB* is wont to add an informative phrase, 'in the

[15] *RSV*[(3)] correctly reads: 'Truly this man was the Son of God.'

words of Scripture' (1 Cor 10²⁰; Eph 5³¹), or 'Scripture says' (1 Cor 15²⁷). But neither version is consistent in the observance of quoted material. Paul's quotation of Deuteronomy 19¹⁵ in 2 Corinthians 13¹, for example, is ignored by both *RSV* and *NEB*.

DIVISIONS OF THE TEXT

NEB retains the verse divisions of 1551, but as marginal indicators, no effort being spared to clear all impediments from before the reader's eyes. We would suggest, however, since the Bible is a major book of reference, that a mark, something like the one used in Nestle (|) be placed in the text to mark the verse division when such division is not obviously marked by punctuation. On the other hand, commentators and producers of concordances must prepare to face the new day that is dawning in the translation of the Bible. Because of the trend towards idiomatic interpretation it is becoming increasingly difficult to maintain an exact correspondence between the material contained in a single Greek verse and that of its English equivalent and it may be necessary to cite the English Bible according to some new division of the text.

CONSISTENCY

To avoid an inflexible consistency, and yet to elude the critic who insists on it—that is the translator's cliff-hanging peril. The British committee, like their American colleagues, and we might add, like their spiritual forbears of 1611, felt free to render the same Greek word by various equivalents. Nor did they feel bound to retain the word or style of the original.

The translators of *NEB* must have known the hazard they were running when they retained a sprinkling of Elizabethan pronouns. Why, after displaying such judicious boldness in almost all other respects in producing a genuinely modern version, they hesitated here, this reader cannot imagine. The inevitable inconsistencies can only annoy even the most favourably impressed reader. Surely it must take a superior exegetical sensitivity to determine that 'Thou' is to be read in Mark 1¹¹ and 'You' in Matthew 25³⁷, ⁴⁵, Presumably Acts 9⁵ is to suggest that Paul is still blind to theological facts. Ananias had been in training and is entitled to say 'thou' (cf. verse 13).

NEB almost consistently shies away from rendering ἰδού, 'behold', with some loss, however, to the reader who will not be able to appreciate the evident attempt, especially in Matthew and Luke, to recreate in the history of Jesus the atmosphere of God's redemptive activity documented in the Old Testament. The word is highly significant in Luke 5[12] and 7[12], to mention but two examples. *RSV* does not hesitate to render 'Behold' but is inconsistent in the retention. In one of the most familiar and dramatic passages, for no accountable reason, *RSV* resorts to a banal 'Here is the man!' (Jn 19[5]). On the other hand, 'Behold' is used to render ἰδέ in verse 4. *NEB* more accurately expresses verse 4 with the 'Here he is', and renders verse 5: 'Behold the Man!' In verse 14, on the other hand, both versions tersely announce, 'Here is your King' (*RSV* punctuates the latter with an exclamation mark). . . .

NEB's treatment of the word δοῦλος is far more consistent than *RSV*'s, at least in the Gospel of Matthew. In this book *NEB* renders the word with 'servant' in all cases except 20[27]. In 2 Peter, on the other hand, *NEB*, following *RSV*, calls Peter a 'servant' (1[1]) but describes the libertines as 'slaves of corruption' (2[19]). The same word, δοῦλος, is used in both passages. In this case consistency seems demanded by the argument. The way to overcome the undesirable moral slavery is to live as a slave of Jesus Christ. In any event a marginal note ought to acquaint the reader with the data, as *RSV* does in connection with Galatians 1[10] and Colossians 4[12]. In both these passages *NEB* also reads 'servant' but without notation. Modernization and a desire to communicate are laudable goals, but there are stubborn historical facts and hoary antiques like 'kisses of peace', 'shields of faith', 'flaming arrows' (not even Phillips dared to render this with 'flame-throwers'), 'coats of mail', and the like, which simply must become a part of one's general knowledge if one is to appreciate documents. A servant today is not a slave. Slaves were owned like cattle; they possessed no will or identity apart from their masters' objectives. That is exactly what the sacred writers want to acknowledge about their relationship to Jesus Christ, yet without the inhumaneness of the pagan world. A translation cannot make a good Bible dictionary superfluous.

We find the *NEB* consistently capitalizes the word 'Law' when νόμος is associated with 'the prophets', as in Matthew 5[17]. The word 'Law' also appears alone in the capitalized form in Luke 2[22], John 12[34], Romans 2[22], but not in Matthew 15[6], Luke 2[23-4],

John 8¹⁷, 10³⁴, 18³¹, Romans 2¹⁷. Inconsistencies of this type should be carefully examined by the editors of a subsequent edition.

In *NEB*, the phrase, οὐ θέλω δὲ ὑμᾶς ἀγνοεῖν (Rom 1¹³, 11²⁵, 1 Cor 10¹, 2 Cor 1⁸) is rendered affirmatively, except in 1 Corinthians 12¹. The latter looks like a clerical slip, in view of the obvious attempt at consistency, but Paul's vigorous style might just as well have been preserved in the other instances, meiosis being one of Paul's favourite devices. On the other hand, *de gustibus* . . ., and the savant can always find healing balm for his offended philological sensibilities in the original.

NEB consistently transposes the pronoun 'I', which in the New Testament frequently appears in a list of two or more personalities (see e.g. 1 Cor 9⁶ and Jn 10³⁰). *RSV* had followed the same procedure, but inconsistently retained 'I and the Father' in the Johannine passage.

Some readers of *NEB* may object that in addition to the name 'Christ', the term 'Messiah' is used to render the word Χριστός. The variation is not itself reprehensible, since the word 'Christ' has for us more of the force of a proper name than for the earliest readers of the Greek New Testament. However, the committee should have made up their minds about such passages as Acts 2³⁸ and 10⁴⁸.

We like the sound of 'Whitsuntide' in 1 Corinthians 16⁸, but are suspicious of any claim on the part of a translator to be able to sense a distinction in Luke's reference to 'Pentecost' (Acts 2¹). Does the Pauline usage document an early liturgical trend in Hellenistic communities?

As we look at the question of consistency we note that *RSV* frequently lapses into unmodernized expressions. *NEB*, generally speaking, avoids this pitfall, but should revaluate its approach to the archaic and especially reassess its treatment of words like δοῦλος and ἰδού.

The question of consistency in notation of divergent renderings and textual variants is of another order. We have observed that neither *RSV* nor *NEB* reveal in these areas consistent patterns. How much is to be included in a work designed primarily for lay consumption? It is conceivable that were scholars to be served, the margins would obliterate the text. It might be well to recall the words of Miles Smith. 'Why', he queried, 'weary the unlearned, who need not so much, and trouble the learned, who know it already?' The editors of both *RSV* and *NEB* have generally exercised a wise judgement in their use of the margins. Pastors and students always have recourse to the primary sources.

SUMMARY

It is indeed a privilege accorded to no other age, that in a brief space of time we should enjoy two such permanently significant religious publications as *RSV* and *NEB*. Both versions come at a time when biblical scholarship has found so much to share. Both versions earnestly endeavour to communicate in clear idiomatic English, but in all honesty we must admit that the *RSV* translators were hampered by the directive to retain a reasonable facsimile of the *KJV* and its descendants. Again, this is not said in criticism of the illustrious scholars responsible for *RSV* but rather of the thinking that lay behind its production. The *KJV* is a venerable old lady and can stand on her own dignity. Periodic beauty treatment and layers of interpretative cosmetics can only dim her distinctive charm.

And that a refurbishing of the ancient lustre has not satisfied the demands of our generation is evident from the fact that many who pay lip-service to *RSV* resort to modern-speech versions of the New Testament, especially the rendering by J. B. Phillips. The British translators have taken a bold but necessary step, and in their translation all students of the New Testament, both lay and professional, pewman and pulpitman, have a rendering which meets all ordinary needs. The watchful eyes and sensitive ears of a special committee of experts in the English language have insured this version against the banal and pedestrian. Only a Homer could dare to put the Siren's song in writing, and who would have thought that the Elizabethan version of John 14–17 could have been matched if not surpassed in poignant words of English beauty? Many of its cadenced phrases will become a part of tomorrow's literary expression. 'Do not feed your pearls to pigs' (Mt 7[6]). 'The love of Christ leaves us no choice' (2 Cor 5[14]). 'How blest are those whose hearts are pure!' (Mat 5[8]). 'They were too good for this world' (Heb 11[38]). All one-syllable words, cleanly hewn. Here is modern speech, tomorrow's idiom and liturgical rhythm in rare combination.

Some there are who will object to a few British expressions that add distinctive flavour here and there. It is our impression that alleged intrusion of provincial patois is greatly exaggerated. The fact is that in most cases the British committee have used English diction precisely, and our own ears are not so sensitive to the precision. *NEB*'s 'incorporate' (as in Eph 1[13]) will offer the American expositor excellent imagery if only he will explore the possibilities. But what about 'fortnight' (Gal 1[18]); 'The people rounded on them' (Mt 20[31]) 'meal-tub' (Mk 4[21]); 'fell foul' (Mk 6[3]); 'appear in the dock' (Phil 1[7]); 'strolling exorcists' (Acts 19[13]); 'pounds' and 'corn' (*passim*) and 'farthing' (Mk 12[42])? No English translation will communicate across the board to all English-speaking nationals, and it is unfair to criticize a translation for not attempting the impossible, nor is the solution an entirely different translation for Americans. If the British translation is to be considered for public use in America then one of two courses seems desirable; either to render British dialect peculiarities into corresponding idiomatic Americanese in an 'authorized' American edition, or to note in the margin the American equivalent of any expressions which might prove an obstacle to the American reader. The publishers, who have displayed such acumen in the promotion of their publication, should be able to take this hurdle in their stride and come up with an appropriate solution. On the other hand, for those who long after the ink-pots of Shakespeare and King James, these occasional expressions may come as a kind of solace.

This new translation, as we have repeatedly observed, will not make obsolete the study of New Testament Greek. Whether he uses this version, *KJV*, or *RSV*, the conscientious pastor must accept the responsibility to compare the version he uses with a critical edition of the Greek text. Despite the lavish care bestowed on even this latest venture, there is so much these ancient authors tried to say, so great the burden on the Spirit's heart, that much spills over the sides of even the most carefully designed interpretative vessel. Yet, we would repeat, this new translation inspires a greater degree of confidence than any of its predecessors in the English language.

We accept with gratitude this first instalment of a noble treasure coming from a nation whose giants of the pen have made the Hall of Literary Fame a place of public meeting, and we hope, in the words of the Preface to the American edition of the *Book of Common Prayer*, that this translation may be 'allowed such just and favourable construction as in common equity ought to be allowed to all human writings'. In this the 350th anniversary year of the publication of the *King James Version* of Sacred Scripture we can pay our British cousins no higher tribute than to say: You have done it again!

Interpretation[1]

PAUL E. DAVIES

... A GOOD TRANSLATION is really a commentary, and in it decisions as to meaning are registered. Consequently, any translation will be subjected to criticism by those who find a different meaning in the passage. We offer a few examples of possible criticism as to the meanings which are put in words.

The word usually translated 'righteousness' in Paul (δικαιοσύνη and its cognates) has a range of usage and meaning in the Greek Testament, and it is rendered here by such terms as 'justice', 'integrity', 'rectitude', 'goodness', 'what God requires', 'a question of morals', and others. We would question the choice of the word 'justice' for δικαιοσύνη in Romans 3²¹: 'God's justice has been brought to light.'

The word ἐκκλησία means 'assembly', 'congregation', 'church'. Tyndale insisted on the use of 'congregation', but his successors came to use 'church'. This translation has used 'congregation' for the local churches but 'church' when referring to the local church in Jerusalem. The usage does not seem to be consistent. Were the translators influenced by the contingent of Congregationalists? Then again in 1 Corinthians, Paul speaks of building up 'the community' (ἐκκλησία).

The translators have pointed up a very interesting distinction between 'Messiah' and 'Christ'. The Greek Testament has only two occurrences of the word 'Messiah' (Jn 1⁴², 4⁴⁵). But in this translation the term 'Christ', where it is used as an official title, is rendered 'Messiah'. 'Christ' is retained where it is the name or the second name, 'Jesus Christ'. The adjustment is most enlightening to the reader.

The word 'Christian' occurs only three times in the Greek Testament. Here it is the translation for 'those that are of the Way', 'those in Christ' or 'those in the Lord', and also 'brothers'. Such broad construing of the terms tends to destroy the distinctive meanings.

[1] Vol. XV, No. 3 (July 1961), pp. 339-44.

The word for 'Gentiles' is also the word for 'nations'. Here it is translated 'Gentiles', 'heathen', 'foreign power', 'the nations', 'the world'. There is a question whether they have consistently retained the term 'Gentiles' for pagan individuals, as distinct from 'the nations' as collective units.

The Greek expression usually rendered 'God forbid' occurs at least fourteen times, and in this translation it is represented by at least nine different phrasings such as 'Certainly not', 'By no means', 'No, no!', 'Of course not', 'I cannot believe it', 'Far from it', 'Never', 'No, Never!' Was this variety necessary to the translation of such a tight, compact expression?

The word ἱλαστήριον and its cognates appear in the older translations in connection with propitiation. In some earlier studies C. H. Dodd has taken the position that these terms refer rather to expiation. It is therefore most interesting to see that 'expiation' and 'remedy for defilement' are used in this translation.

These small details do serve to point up the fact that this new translation should properly be judged in relation to the Greek text, not by comparison with the *King James Version*. The real base of reference and criticism is found in the Greek Testament, and the question to ask is, not how it compares with the *King James* and its revisions (RV and *RSV*, etc.), but whether this new translation is a faithful rendering of the Greek text. On this basis we may point out that at certain points it adds phrases which are not parallel in the Greek, for instance, Romans 3[20], 2 Corinthians 1[24], Galatians 2[17], Ephesians 2[14]. Is this justified in order to secure a clear reading? Or, can the translators justify the very free paraphrase that appears at many points? And on what basis? These references to the Greek Testament lead this reviewer to make the comment that this new translation cannot be judged with any accuracy apart from a knowledge of the New Testament Greek text. . . .

Journal of Biblical Literature[1]

FREDERICK C. GRANT

...SOME OF the outstanding advances in NT translation may be listed here. In Matthew 6[13] the petition in the Lord's Prayer reads, 'And do not bring us to the test', which is clearly what the Greek requires. Ἐισενέγκῃς is not derived from εἰσάγω, as many careless readers assume, but from εἰσφέρω, and it carries a sense of compulsion. Πειρασμός is not 'temptation', in the modern sense, but trial, testing, the kind of trouble that breaks or tries men's souls, under which many of the weak simply fail. (See Sirach 2[1ff]. 'My son, if you come forward to serve the Lord, prepare yourself for temptation' (or trials, *RSV* mg.), i.e. for trouble, as the rest of the passage makes clear.) The *NEB* quite rightly takes this as the sense of the word in the Lord's Prayer, and it will surely be a great relief to many religious-minded persons who simply cannot believe that God ever 'leads into temptation', like some pagan deity—in Homer or Euripides—determined to trick and destroy a hapless mortal. Martin Rinkart's famous hymn, *Nun Danket* (1630), conveys the sense very well. So does the beautiful collect in the Roman Mass, a classic expansion and exposition of the petition:

Libera nos, quaesumus, Domine, ab omnibus malis, praeteritis, praesentibus, et futuris. . . . Da propitius pacem in diebus nostris: ut, ope misericordiae tuae adjuti, et a peccato simus semper liberi et ab omni perturbatione securi.

Another example of first-rate translating is Mark 11[17], where some of the 'Letters to the editor' published in recent newspapers have complained of the disappearance of the traditional 'den of thieves'. Of course, people who view the NT only as an English classic, and prize its antique idioms for their familiarity and their influence on later English writers, feel no concern over inaccuracy

[1] Vol. LXXX, No. 2 (June 1961), pp. 173–6.

or obscurity in rendering or even the religious meaning or interpretation. But σπήλαιον λῃστῶν, simply does not mean 'den of thieves': it is a 'cave of robbers', armed bandits. A 'den of thieves' could be anywhere in some dark alley, in some dingy back room or cellar in seventeenth-century London. But 'robbers cave', especially on Jesus's lips, makes one think at once of those caves in Galilee where bandits (really revolutionists, according to Josephus) hid their loot, until one day Herod, then a young officer out to win his spurs, had himself and his men let down by ropes over the cliff and burned them out.

Not so good is 'tax-gatherers' (e.g. Mt 5⁴⁶). Did they go about on their oppressive mission, or did people come to them, the tax-collectors? (see Mt 9–10). But this is only a trifle. Instead, look at Matthew 7¹¹, where 'ye, being evil' has become 'you, then, bad as you are', which is certainly what Jesus meant. He was not teaching 'the corruption in man's heart', the doctrine of original sin, nor even contrasting men with God, but arguing, in good Jewish style, 'from the less to the greater'. You are fair and honest in dealing with your children: how much the more is God! 'If you then, bad as you are (in most ways), know how to give your children what is good for them, how much more will your heavenly Father give good things to those who ask him!'

Or Matthew 8²⁶, 'Why are you such cowards? . . . how little faith you have!' This is magnificent—like James Moffatt's rendering. Many readers will turn at once to 1 Corinthians 13 for the acid test, and some will still be looking for the 'tinkling cymbal'— though who ever heard a cymbal do that? No: what Paul wrote is what the *NEB* gives us: 'a sounding gong or a clanging cymbal', noisy, strident, but mere empty sound, *vox et praeterea nihil*. Verse 13 is magnificent too: 'In a word, there are three things that last for ever: faith, hope, and love; but the greatest of them all is love.'

Philemon 9 reads 'ambassador'; Revelation 10⁶ has 'no more delay'; 2 Corinthians 5¹⁶ has 'worldly standards . . . in our understanding of Christ'; Hebrews 11¹ has 'Faith gives substance (mg., or assurance) to our hopes, and makes us certain of realities we do not see'; Romans 1¹⁷ reads, 'God's way of righting wrong, a way that starts from faith and ends in faith; as Scripture says, "he shall gain life who is justified through faith"'; John 1¹: 'When all things began, the Word already was. The word dwelt with God, and what

God was, the Word was.' These are but a handful of *cruces interpretum* (which means *interpretation* expressed in a *translation*) and they are, I think, fairly representative of the book. One could easily supply a dozen more—or several dozen. The work is extremely well done, and will be in use for generations to come. It does not take the place—no translation can ever take the place—of careful study of the original. But for those who do not know Greek, this translation is sure to provide a vivid, fresh experience in understanding the NT writings. . . .

Princeton Seminary Bulletin[1]

BRUCE M. METZGER

THE RECURRING NEED FOR REVISIONS

...THE RECURRING need for new translations of the Bible arises from several circumstances. The three which are most important relate to (*a*) advances made in lower (or textual) criticism of the New Testament manuscripts, (*b*) the acquisition of more precise information as to the meaning of Greek words and syntax, and (*c*) changes in the usage of the English language. The first is obviously the most basic of these three, for without textual criticism one does not know which variant reading deserves to be regarded as the original text. ...

After the Greek text has been established in its purest form, the translator must make every effort to understand the meaning of its words and phrases. Here the Panel of translators utilized the advances made by scholars during the past two generations. The discovery at the beginning of the twentieth century of many thousands of papyrus documents in the everyday Greek of the New Testament period has made possible a better appreciation of the finer shades of meaning of more than one Greek word or phrase in the New Testament. ...

It is chiefly in the third area mentioned above that the special characteristics of the new version are to be found, namely the set purpose to break with all previous translations and to make a free translation into the English of today. ...

The accommodation to modern idiom is to be seen in such details as the altering of the sequence of items when the first person is involved. It will be remembered that Near Eastern custom gives priority to the first person (seen, for example, in what has come to be called the Mizpah benediction, 'The Lord watch between *me* and thee. ...'), whereas our contemporary usage prefers to put oneself last in a series. Accordingly, the new translation transfers the sequence of the Greek and previous English translations to

[1] Vol. LV, No. 1 (September 1961), pp. 56–63.

F

read, 'My father and I are one' (Jn 10³⁰). Similarly, instead of saying '[they] gave me and Barnabas the right hand of fellowship' (Gal 2⁹), the new version renders the passage '[they] accepted Barnabas and myself as partners, and shook hands upon it'—the latter clause of which is a rather anachronistic expression to foist upon first-century Near Easterners.

The translators of the new version have not hesitated to encroach upon the field of the commentator and to paraphrase the text when they believed that a literal rendering would be less satisfactory. Thus, in the passage from John quoted above, twice the word κόσμος has been translated 'godless world.' The following are other examples of the insertion of words for which there is no express warrant in the text (for convenience of explanation the inserted words are italicized here; they are not italicized in the new version): 'Those who sleep *in death*' (1 Thess. 4¹³); 'in the *province* of Asia' (Rev 1⁴); 'in his body of flesh *and blood*' (Col 1²²); '*guardian* angel' (Mt 18¹⁰, Acts 12¹⁵); '*human* body' (Rom 12⁴); '*his life's* blood' (Rev 1⁵); 'tongues of *ecstasy*' (1 Cor 13⁸). In other cases the literal rendering is supplanted altogether by a periphrasis; thus 'scribes' become 'doctors of the law' (Mk 15³¹, etc.), the parable of the talents is now the parable of the bags of gold (Mt 25¹⁴⁻³⁰); the word traditionally translated 'saints' is rendered 'God's people' (Col 1², etc.); 'beloved' as a term of address becomes 'dear friends' (1 John 4⁷, etc.); and the verb 'it is written' (Rom 12¹⁹) becomes 'there is a text which reads'. Instances of this kind of paraphrase could be multiplied. . . .

Though the translators were instructed to make an entirely new translation, it is perhaps inevitable that here and there one can detect echoes of felicitous turns of expression borrowed from earlier versions. The striking phrase, he who 'brought life and immortality to light through the Gospel' (2 Tim 1¹⁰), comes straight from the *KJV* and *RSV*. In Romans 16⁴, Prisca and Aquila are said to have 'risked their necks' to save Paul's life, just as in the *RSV*. There are other passages where, instead of striving to be different, the British Committee would have been well advised to adopt a forceful earlier rendering. Thus, in 1 John 5⁴, 'The victory that defeats the world is our faith', strikes one as a distinctly weaker translation than the traditional '. . . that overcomes the world . . .'. And the crisp, though familiar, translation of Jesus's agraphon, 'It is more blessed to give than to receive'

(Acts 20[35]), is supplanted by the inferior English: 'Happiness lies more in giving than in receiving.'

A certain unevenness of translation and, indeed, diversity of orientation can be observed in the several parts of the New Testament. For example, in Ephesians and Revelation, ἐκκλησία is regularly translated by 'church'. In the other books it is translated 49 times by 'congregation' and 21 times by 'church'. Likewise, a curious vacillation can be observed even within the same book regarding the presence or absence of capital letters. For example, one finds 'Gospel' in Romans 1[1], but in 1[2] it is spelled 'gospel', as also in 1[9]; but in 1[16] it is printed with an upper-case initial letter. In Matthew 'Bar-Abbas' appears four times, but in Mark, Luke, and John the word is spelled 'Barabbas'.

Finally, attention may be called to one or two blatant errors in the new version which have escaped the vigilance of the Committee. In most manuscripts, Matthew 9[34] reads, 'But the Pharisees said, "He casts out devils by the prince of devils"', but a few ancient witnesses omit the verse entirely. Misinterpreting the textual evidence, the British translators erroneously divide the sentence, putting part of it in the text ('He casts out devils by the prince of devils'), and part of it in a footnote ('*Some witnesses read* But the Pharisees said, "He casts out devils . . ." '). This is a blunder for the manuscript evidence requires that the sentence be treated as a whole and placed either entirely in the text or entirely in a footnote. Another error appears at 1 John 2[13], which reads, 'I write to you, fathers, because you know him who is and has been from the beginning', with a footnote attached to the last word, reading, 'Or him whom we have known from the beginning'. There is no justification for translating the Greek as is done in this alternative rendering. . . .

Times Literary Supplement[1]

...THE *New English Bible: New Testament* is born into a highly competitive world. How does it compare with its rivals?

First, the underlying Greek Text.

The Authorized Version was based on the so-called 'Received Text'—that is, on the text represented by the majority of Greek manuscripts then known and for that reason generally accepted. But progress in textual studies gradually made it plain that reliance on mere numbers was a delusion. The manuscripts containing the Received Text were uniformly late in date and therefore witnesses to a type of text likely to be more reliable than some other types of text identifiable in other, much earlier, manuscripts. The Cambridge scholars Westcott and Hort, in the sixth and seventh decades of the last century, identified three main types of text; and one of these, the 'Neutral Text' (represented pre-eminently by the two great fourth-century manuscripts Vaticanus and Sinaiticus), they thought approximated very closely to the New Testament originals.

Westcott and Hort were both members of the New Testament Revision Panel appointed in 1870; and it was only natural that the Revised Version of 1881 should very largely reflect their textual theory. Thus, at Mark 9²⁹ the Revised Version omits the words 'and fasting', because they are not found in the oldest, 'Neutral' manuscripts. And omissions of this kind are frequent, sometimes amounting to whole verses (e.g. Acts 8³⁷). Not that Westcott and Hort had it all their own way, as can be seen by comparing the Revised Version with their own published Greek text. But a high proportion of their proposals were accepted, and most of those that were not had attention drawn to them in the many marginal notes, so characteristic of this version, which refer to the 'ancient authorities'.

Since the days of Westcott and Hort many more 'ancient authorities' have been discovered and a number of additional

[1] No. 3082 (24th March 1961), pp. 177-8.

types of text identified. The whole problem has, in consequence, become much more complex; and no textual critic today would be prepared to follow unreservedly any one type of text throughout the New Testament any more than he would be prepared to rely exclusively on any single manuscript. Modern opinion favours an 'eclectic' approach, which means in practice that each particular reading in each particular instance is judged on its merits and not by rule of thumb. It is this 'eclectic' approach which has been adopted by the translators of the *New English Bible* just as it was adopted by the translators of the *Revised Standard Version*. Differences between these two groups of translators, each of which was working on the same general principles, are therefore as interesting to note as are the differences of both from their predecessors.

So far as the RV's excisions and omissions from the AV are concerned both the *RSV* and the *New English Bible* agree almost always in support of the RV: indeed, they may be said to have carried the process initiated by the RV a stage farther—thus, Luke 22^{19b-20}, which still forms part of the text in the RV, is relegated to the margin in both the *RSV* and the *New English Bible*. Examples of other agreements against the RV are 'Judaea' for 'Galilee' at Luke 4^{44} and 'good things already in being' for 'good things to come' at Hebrews 9^{11}. In all these instances the RV follows the AV. When the RV and the AV differ, the two modern versions sometimes agree in going behind the RV and preferring the reading of the AV, as when they prefer ἀπάταις ('deceptions') for ἀγάπαις ('love-feasts') at 2 Peter 2^{13}, or πέπωκαν ('have drunk deep of') for πέπτωκαν ('are fallen') at Revelation 28^3.

But the *RSV* and the *New English Bible* by no means always agree in their choice of readings: in the first verse of Ephesians, for instance, the words 'at Ephesus' are rejected by the *RSV*, but retained in the new version. A detailed comparison, however, shows that the translators have generally been rather more adventurous than were the Americans, especially in their acceptance of so-called 'Western' readings, such as ὀργισθείς ('in warm indignation') for σπλαγχνισθείς ('moved with pity') at Mark 1^{41}, Δουβέριος ('the Doberian') for Δερβαῖος ('of Derbe') at Acts 20^4, and ἀνθρώπινος ('popular') for πιστός ('sure') at 1 Timothy 3^1.

Examination of the footnotes confirms this conclusion. The note at Matthew 6^{28} draws attention to the recently discovered original reading of *Sinaiticus* ('Consider the lilies: they neither card nor spin, nor labour'), while that on 'Mary' at Luke 1⁴⁶ runs: *So the majority of ancient witnesses: some read* Elizabeth: *the original may have had no name.* From this last note one gets the impression that a sizable majority of the translators would have liked very much to 'have had no name' in their translations, and so, by implication, to have referred the *Magnificat* to Elizabeth. Yet the *RSV* has no note at all here. Nor has it a note at Matthew 6²⁸.

Naturally, many of the readings accepted will be questioned. The omission of 'But the Pharisees said' at Matthew 9³⁴, for example, alters the sense of the entire passage. What is the evidence for the omission of these words in this verse only? And if it be thought compelling, is there not an equally good, or better, case for omitting 'the poor are hearing the good news' two chapters later in Matthew 11⁵? In the latter passage there is not only very respectable manuscript evidence for the omission: stylistic considerations also suggest that the words have been interpolated from the parallel passage in Luke 7²². Such questions as these inevitably arise if one adopts the 'eclectic' approach in textual matters. But all things considered, there is little reasonable ground for complaint. Underneath the *New English Bible* lies a Greek text that is as good as any that can be constructed in existing circumstances.

'In doing our work', the translators write, 'we have constantly striven to follow our instructions and render the Greek, as we understood it, into the English of the present day, that is, into the natural vocabulary, constructions, and rhythms of contemporary speech. We have sought to avoid archaism, jargon, and all that is either stilted or slipshod. . . . Always the overriding aims were accuracy and clarity.' How successful they have been may be best appreciated by setting their new version alongside the Authorized Version, the Revised Version, and the *Revised Standard Version*. A good illustrative verse for this purpose is Revelation 13¹⁸.

AV
Here is wisdom. Let him that hath understanding count the number of the beast; for it is the number of a man; and his number is Six hundred threescore and six.

RV

Here is wisdom. He that hath understanding, let him count the number of the beast: for it is the number of a man: and his number is Six hundred and sixty and six.

RSV

This calls for wisdom: let him who has understanding reckon the number of the beast, for it is a human number, its number is six hundred and sixty-six.

NEB

Here is the key; and anyone who has intelligence may work out the number of the beast. The number represents a man's name, and the numerical value of its letters is six hundred and sixty-six.

There can be no doubt about which of these four extracts is the most 'contemporary', and which, therefore, in the given 'contemporary' context, is the best.

The translators also tell us that their 'intention has been to offer a translation in the strict sense, and not a paraphrase', and that they have taken 'the liberty of introducing into a passage something which is not there, to elucidate the meaning which is there . . . only with extreme caution, and in a very few passages'. Many readers will beg to differ. In the quotation of Revelation 13[18] above, 'The number represents a man's name, and the numerical value of its letters . . .' is patently an example of 'introducing into a passage something which is not there, to elucidate the meaning which is there'. 'Bags of gold' for 'talents' at Matthew 25[15ff], is another example; 'guardian angels' for 'angels' at Matthew 18[10] and Acts 12[15] another; 'a testament, or covenant' at Galatians 3[17] another. And so one might go on. Not that there is anything improper in any of these expansions, if the primary concern is the elucidation of meaning. What is important is that the unwary should not be misled into thinking that they are less frequent than they are, and that the translation generally is less free than in fact it is.

Long and involved Greek sentences are regularly broken up— and sometimes sentences that are not so long. Impersonal third-person plurals are turned into passives, verbal phrases into substantival, and substantival into verbal. Thus, the familiar

'Thou sayest' (Mk 15²) becomes 'The words are yours', and the Prologue to John opens:

When all things began, the Word already was. The Word dwelt with God, and what God was, the Word was. The Word, then, was with God at the beginning, and through him all things came to be.

This last extract illustrates also another characteristic of the version—its predilection for variety. The two phrases 'When all things began' and 'at the beginning' represent only one Greek phrase (ἐν ἀρχῇ) repeated; yet the translators have no hesitation in rendering it differently in adjacent verses. On the same principle, though in different books, 'heaven' is 'opened' or 'wide open' in the Gospels (Mt 3¹⁶, Lk 3²¹, Jn 1⁵¹), but there is 'a rift in the sky' in Acts (7⁵⁶, 10¹¹).

No one will be so foolish as to maintain that the same Greek word must always mean the same thing regardless of context, or deny that a modicum of variation is therefore necessary (the word παῖς in the Centurion's plea 'εἰπὲ λόγῳ καὶ ἰαθήσεται ὁ παῖς μου' is quite rightly rendered 'boy' at Matthew 8⁸, but 'servant' at Luke 7⁷). Yet the translators of the new version have in general so far outstripped 'King James's men' in the exhibition of 'the wholesome practice' of variation as to make their appeal to their predecessors' preface beside the point. For instance, γραμματεῖς (=sopherim) are mentioned in the New Testament altogether sixty-one times: each time the AV (followed by the RV and *RSV*) renders 'scribes'; but the *New English Bible* gives 'lawyers' thirty times, 'doctors of the law' twenty-five times, 'teachers' four times, and 'teachers of the law' twice. There is no discernible rationale behind these variations. Variety, it would seem, is a virtue in itself.

Γραμματεῖς, of course, is an ancient Jewish technical term in Greek; and all technical terms are notoriously difficult to translate. Some of these technical terms, mostly the more theological, the translators have made no attempt to render into modern idiom: they have been content, very wisely, to leave them in their traditional dress (e.g. 'the Holy Place', 'Grace', 'The Day of the Lord'). But that they have done so raises acutely the question whether it is possible to produce a really up-to-date New Testament and further, if it were possible, whether from the Christian point of view it would be anything like as desirable as is commonly supposed.

In the modern world the fundamental ideas of the New Testament are as antiquated, alien, and 'irrelevant', as is the language of the Authorized Version. Yet these are the ideas into which the Church is commissioned to baptize the world in every age. And there are no adequate grounds for thinking that mere modernization of the language in which they are expressed will make them either more up to date essentially or more acceptable universally.

If we grant that in the *New English Bible* we are offered the most satisfactory modern version of the New Testament available, what are its prospects?

There are conservatives who have already committed themselves in advance to faithfulness to the Authorized Version: with them the new version will make little headway. At the other extreme, those who, after the manner of St Luke's Athenians, have 'no time for anything but talking or hearing about the latest novelty' in biblical matters will welcome it with open arms. Most of those who habitually read the Bible will give it at least a trial, as will also some who do not. Besides this we shall hear it read in church. At first it will sound strange, and to many faintly improper. But in time we shall get used to the Parable of 'the Dishonest Bailiff', to 'Blood Acre', as the name of the 'property' that Judas bought, and to St Paul sending his 'love to you all' at Corinth. It is then that the real test will come. When the interest surrounding its publication has evaporated, when the novelty has worn off, and when the initial shocks have been absorbed, how will the new version fare?

The opinion has been expressed that in a few years' time there will be two versions only in normal use in this country—the Authorized Version and the *New English Bible*: the Revised Version, it is suggested, will quietly disappear (and with it, presumably, the *Revised Standard Version*). For reading in church this may well be so. Perhaps also for private reading. But hardly for Bible-study.

Bible students who are well versed in Greek will doubtless resort to the new version frequently as a storehouse of sound scholarly opinion, even though they are not in need of a version in the ordinary way. But there is an increasing number of Bible students today who know either no Greek or very little Greek. For them a reliable English version is a necessity. And it is here that the *New English Bible* conspicuously fails. Not that its accuracy can be questioned or its scholarship impugned. It is simply that the basic principles on which the translators have worked make it a far less satisfactory text for the student who is weak in Greek than the otherwise much inferior Revised and *Revised Standard* Versions.

'The older translators, on the whole, considered that fidelity to the original demanded that they should reproduce, as far as possible, characteristic features of the language in which it was written. . . . The present translators were enjoined to replace Greek constructions and idioms by those of contemporary English.' They have certainly done so—and with no mean success. But in doing so they have largely 'ironed out' what is distinctive as between one part of the New Testament and another. St James in 'contemporary English' sounds very much more like St Paul than ever he did before; and the differences in style between the Prologue to St Luke's Gospel, the same evangelist's account of the birth of John the Baptist, and a specimen narrative chapter from the end of Acts are correspondingly less striking in the new version than they are in the earlier versions. For the Greekless Bible student this is a serious loss.

The new version's predilection for variety has been noted already. In their introduction the translators admit to having felt under no obligation to translate the same Greek word everywhere by the same English word, and they have varied their rendering accordingly. What they do not go on to admit is that they have felt under no obligation to translate different Greek words by different English words either. Confusion thus becomes even worse confounded. As we have seen, γραμματεῖς as a technical term for the Jewish '*sopherim*' is rendered in four different ways. But St Luke, alone among the evangelists, uses not only γραμματεῖς for the '*sopherim*', but also νομικοί; and his alternation between the two is usually thought to have a bearing on the problem of his sources. In the AV, the RV, and the *RSV*, γραμματεῖς is regularly rendered throughout Luke by 'scribes', and νομικοί by 'lawyers'; it is therefore clear in any one instance which term is used in the original. But in the *New English Bible* 'lawyers' may stand for either γραμματεῖς or νομικοί, and the Greekless have no means of determining which.

This kind of confusion is even more obvious, and more disconcerting, in the parallel passages in the Gospels. For example, in

Matthew 5²⁵⁻⁶ and Luke 12⁵⁸⁻⁹ 'ὁ ἀντίδικος σου' is rendered by 'someone' who 'sues you' in Matthew, but in Luke by 'your opponent': the same word 'farthing' in English does duty for two Greek words—'κοδράντης' in Matthew and 'λεπτόν' in Luke; and the difference between 'ἀμὴν λέγω σοι, οὐ μὴ ἐξέλθῃς ἐκεῖθεν' and 'λέγω σοι, οὐ μὴ ἐξέλθῃς ἐκεῖθεν' (i.e. a difference only between the presence and absence of 'ἀμήν') is represented by the difference between 'I tell you, once you are there you will not be let out' and 'I tell you, you will not come out'. Or again, at Luke 5²⁹ we are told that 'ὄχλος πολὺς τελωνῶν καὶ ἄλλων' sat down with our Lord at table. This is rendered, unexceptionably, 'a large party of tax-gatherers and others'. But in the two parallel passages (Mt 9¹⁰ and Mark 2¹⁵) the Greek runs 'πολλοὶ τελῶναι καὶ ἁμαρτωλοί', which is rendered in both passages, 'many bad characters—tax-gatherers and others'. (The literal rendering is 'many tax-gatherers and sinners'.) The 'and others' in Matthew and Mark is very odd indeed. Can it be an unconscious assimilation to Luke? Is the whole phrase, therefore, what Westcott and Hort might have called 'a conflate rendering'?

It will be clear from the examples given that it is impossible to discover anything in detail from the new version about the relationship between one Gospel and another. Yet it is precisely this sort of thing that the Greekless Bible student requires from a version. He will find it in the Revised Version: he will find it also in the *Revised Standard Version*; and, it may be added, in the Authorized Version, far more readily than he ever will in the new version.

The new version has its merits. That no one will wish to deny. If one's sole concern is with what the New Testament writers mean, it is excellent. It is otherwise if one wants to find out what the documents actually say.

Journal of Bible and Religion[1]

BRUCE H. THROCKMORTON, JR.

... OF COURSE, one's estimate of the new translation will depend on the tests one puts to it, the criteria by which it is judged, and the purpose one expects it to serve. A translation may fail according to some criteria but be successful according to others. We should not make the mistake of assuming either that one attribute (important though it may be) means total success or that one weakness (pervasive though it may be) means utter failure. In what follows we shall consider several different aspects of this new translation, often comparing it with the *RSV* and *KJV*, in order to shed light from more than one point of view.

TEXT

(a) *Variant Readings*

There are, of course, no original manuscripts of the New Testament, but simply thousands of manuscripts whose readings often differ from one another. A translator must decide in each case where there are so-called 'variant readings' which reading he will accept as the original and use as the basis of his translation. One of the interesting aspects of the *NEB* is that it reveals a refreshing and sometimes quite daring willingness on the part of its translators to choose what seemed to them the best text, regardless of the resulting necessity of departing frequently from the traditional English translation. The Greek text presupposed by the *NEB* is an eclectic one, as it should be. It is far more eclectic than that presupposed in the *RSV*, which version is fairly conservative in its departures from traditional readings. We should observe also that the *NEB* includes translations of many alternative texts in the footnotes. In fact, virtually all the footnotes are either translations of alternative readings or alternative translations of the same reading, of which there are also many. The footnotes contain no biblical references at all, to either Testament.

[1] Vol. XXIX (July 1961), pp. 193–203.

When alternative texts are translated in the footnotes, judgements are not made as to the kind of support available either for the text adopted, or for alternative texts. The usual notation is simply: 'Some witnesses read', or 'add', or 'insert', or 'omit'. Or, 'Other witnesses read'; or, in nine places, 'One witness reads'. This practice is laudable. But, why, then, 'One *early* witness has' (p. 3); 'Some *ancient* witnesses read' (pp. 126, 278); '*Many* witnesses read' (p. 123); and 'So the majority of *ancient* witnesses' (p. 94)? These adjectives (*early, ancient* and *many*) are scrupulously avoided elsewhere.

The translation of selected 'variant readings' is a very helpful practice, but some of the texts so translated seem hardly necessary in the light of other omissions. For example, at Mark 10⁴⁰ the relatively inconsequential reading 'by my Father' is translated (words that are clearly a later addition to Mark, made by assimilation to Matthew 20²³ and in no way altering or adding to Mark's meaning); but the longer reading of Acts 8³⁹, which is of considerable interest and significance, is not disclosed. The so-called 'Western non-interpolations' of Luke 22 and 24 are all in the footnotes, except at Luke 24³ where there is no note for the reading, 'of the Lord Jesus'.

The interpolation in John concerning Jesus and the adulterous woman (Jn 7⁵³–8¹¹) is handled very nicely; it is placed on a separate page at the end of the Gospel. Mark 16⁹⁻²⁰ and the 'Shorter Ending' of Mark are not relegated to smaller type in footnotes (as in *RSV*); they are left as part of the text, the shorter ending being placed before verse 9, with a note indicating that 'some of the most ancient witnesses' close Mark at 16⁸. The so-called 'Freer Ending' is not mentioned.

In his review of the *RSV* in *The Journal of Biblical Literature*[2] Kendrick Grobel raises the question of the meaning and value of providing translations of 'variant readings' if support is omitted for both 'variants' and the readings adopted. Surely a reader sufficiently interested in the text to bother with a 'variant reading' in the footnotes would also want to have some indication of the textual evidence for the readings involved. He might like to know, for example, that the 'one witness' whose reading is adopted at John 19²⁹ is an eleventh-century cursive, and not a second- or third-century papyrus reading. Indeed, he deserves to be told what

[2] LXVI.4 (December 1947). 361ff.

the 'one witness' is; if some readers are not interested, nothing is lost. Once time and space are taken to provide textual data, they should also be given up to making such data intelligible. As matters stand, the reader is provided no way of interpreting the significance of the data offered him.

(b) *Examples of Textual Readings*

Following are illustrations of the non-traditional, eclectic character of the *NEB* text—readings not preferred or adopted in *RSV*, or in the Greek texts of Nestle or Westcott and Hort (unless otherwise noted):

Matthew 1^{10}, *Amon* (rather than *Amos*); 1^{18} omits *Jesus* (W.H. brackets); 9^{34} omits *But the Pharisees said*, and retains the rest of the verse; 10^3, *Lebbaeus* (rather than *Thaddaeus*); 12^{47}, verse included, with no footnote (Nestle brackets); 13^{35}, 'prophecy of *Isaiah*'; 14^{30} adds *strong* (with *wind*); 15^6, *law* (rather than *word*); 16^{2b-3} omitted (bracketed in Nestle and W.H.); 22^{35} omits *a lawyer*; $27^{16, 17}$, *Jesus Bar-Abbas*.

Mark 1^{41} reads Gk. ὀργισθείς (weakly translated *in warm indignation*), rather than reading Gk. for *moved with pity*; 8^{26}, 'Do not *tell anyone in* the village'; 8^{38a}, 'If anyone is ashamed of me and *mine*; 8^{38b}, 'in the glory of his Father *and of* the holy angels'; 10^2 omits *Pharisees* (W.H. brackets).

Luke 5^8, *Simon* (rather than *Simon Peter*); $8^{26, 37}$ *Gergesenes*; 9^{26}, 'whoever is ashamed of me and *mine*'; 10^{22}, prefixed by 'Then turning to his disciples he said'; 11^{33} omits *or under a bushel*; 15^{16}, 'glad to *fill his belly* with the pods' (as Nestle); 18^{11}, *The Pharisee stood up and prayed thus:* 22^{16}, 'never again shall I eat it' (as Nestle); 22^{62}, verse omitted (W.H. bracket; *RSV* includes in text, with no footnote); 23^{42}, 'when you come *to your throne*' (as Nestle and W.H.).

John 1^{34}, 'This is *God's Chosen One*'; 3^{13} adds *whose home is in heaven*: 5^2, *Bethesda*: 13^{10} omits *except the feet* (Nestle and W.H. bracket); 16^{23}, *in my name* taken with *ask*, rather than with *give*; $17^{11, 12}$, *which thou hast given me* taken with *them*, rather than with *name*; 19^{29}, *javelin* (rather than *hyssop*).

Acts 1^{26}, *was then assigned a place among the twelve apostles*; 2^{37} omits *the rest of*; 3^{21} omits *from of old*; 4^6, *Jonathan* (for *John*); 11^{11}, 'house where *I* was staying'; 11^{12} ends verse at *told me to go with them*; 18²⁶, *the new way* (rather than *the way of God*); 20⁴, *Gaius the Doberian.*

Romans 5¹, *let us continue at peace* (reading the subjunctive, as W.H.); 8²⁴ᶜ reads Gk. ὑπομένει: 'why should a man *endure and wait for* (rather than *hope for*) what he already sees ?'

1 Corinthians 1¹⁴, *Thank* God (rather than *I am thankful*); 8³ omits *God*; 8¹² omits Gk. ἀσθενοῦσαν (*RSV* trans. *when it is weak*); 14³⁸ᵇ, *he himself should not be recognized*; 15⁵⁴ᵃ omits *the perishable being clothed with the imperishable* (as W.H.).

Galatians 1⁶ omits *of Christ*; 4²⁵ omits *Hagar*, and reads, 'Sinai is a mountain in Arabia.'

Ephesians 5¹⁹ omits *spiritual*. Philippians 3³ omits *God*. 1 Timothy 5¹⁶, 'if a Christian *man or* woman'.

Thus the *NEB* shows a most commendable willingness to break with many traditional readings, and to adopt texts often unanimously rejected (or at least not preferred) by the *RSV*, Nestle and Westcott and Hort. Not everyone will agree, of course, that all the changes are improvements; but the British translators were in many more instances more willing than the American revisers to adopt what they considered to be the best text, even though its reading was quite untraditional, and to break with reliance upon manuscripts that in recent decades have carried great weight.

However, one suspects that in a few instances the translators failed to act according to their best judgement and instead succumbed to the weight of tradition. Whatever the explanation, Luke 22⁴³⁻⁴ and 23³⁴ remain in the text, as do the words *at Ephesus* in Ephesians 1¹; but it is doubtful that only textual judgements were involved. And highly dubious is the text adopted at 1 Corinthians 13³, where *burnt* is read (Gk. καυθήσωμαι, rather than καυχήσωμαι). This is all the more surprising in the light of the translators' regular preference for the Pauline readings of P⁴⁶; the reading here of P⁴⁶ is not *burn*, but *boast* or *glory*. (P⁴⁶ also omits *at Ephesus* in Ephesians 1¹.)

Finally, the translators should certainly have added a note at Philemon verse 9, indicating that the Greek word translated *ambassador* actually means *old man* (the former translation being arrived at only by a conjectured emendation in the spelling of the Greek).

TRANSLATION

We come now to the fundamental matter of the actual translation. As remarked above, we must consider the translation from more than one point of view if our estimate is to be of any value. Following are some reactions to different facets of the new translation, arranged in a quite arbitrary order.

(a) *Contemporaneousness*

The *NEB* Introduction speaks of the desire of the translators to use 'the current speech of our time', 'the idiom of contemporary English'. Have the translators succeeded ? On the whole the answer is yes. . . .

(b) *Accuracy*

The Introduction to the *NEB* states that the translators' 'overriding aims were accuracy and clarity'. I have spoken briefly, and shall speak again, about the matter of clarity. On the question of accuracy we may say that the NEB frequently achieves a heartening degree of accuracy in many places where the *RSV* failed to do so. Often this is due to the close attention paid by the new translators to Greek syntax. Some examples follow:

(1) *Periphrastic Semitisms*, which often are not translated into our idiom in the *RSV*, are handled better in the *NEB*. In the following illustrations, the first translation is *RSV*, the second is *NEB*.

> 'Hell of fire' (Mt 5²², 18⁹) is 'fires of hell'; 'horn of salvation' (Lk 1⁶⁹), which goes back to Tyndale, is 'a deliverer of victorious power'; 'son of perdition' (Jn 17¹², 2 Thess 2³), which was Wyclif's translation (in John, Tyndale translated 'that lost child'), is 'the man who must be lost' in John, and 'the man doomed to perdition' in 2 Thessalonians.

Just why the same Greek expression is translated in two different ways here is not clear, but it is characteristic of the *NEB* as a whole as we shall see later.

'Spirit of stupor' (Rom 11⁸), which is also the *ASV* rendering, becomes, happily, 'numbness of spirit'; 'we were . . . children of wrath' (Eph 2^3), which was Tyndale's translation, is 'we . . . lay under the dreadful judgement of God'; 'sons of disobedience' (Eph 5^6) is 'rebel subjects'; and cf. the translations in Luke 10^6 and 20^{34}.

(2) *Syntax.* The British translators are to be commended on the number of instances in which they have successfully captured the distinction between durative and punctiliar action. The Greek imperfect tense is notoriously difficult to translate, but in many cases the *NEB* renders its significance faithfully, and, on occasion, even brilliantly. The translation of ἔλεγον as 'people were saying' (Mk 3^{21}, 6^{14}, etc.) is just right. So also is the tradition of the following descriptive imperfects: 'Meanwhile he was looking around' (Mk 5^{32}); 'How dearly he must have loved him!' (Jn 11^{36}); and 'we had been hoping' (Lk 24^{21}). But in other instances the significance of the imperfect is not brought out; cf. Mt $3^{5, \ 6}$, 4^{11}, 13^8, Mk 14^{35}, Lk 2^{49}, 10^{18}.

Compare the following translations of iterative (customary) imperfects with the *RSV* renderings, noting how admirably *NEB* realizes their durative force: 'It was the practice of his parents to go to Jerusalem every year' (Lk 2^{41}); 'he was . . . breaking the Sabbath' (Jn 5^{18}); 'used to be carried there and laid every day' (Acts 3^2), 'which you always had before you' (1 Jn 2^7). But, once again, the sense of these imperfects is not caught in other passages, such as Mk 7^{26}, 11^{19}, Lk 5^{15}, Jn 3^{22}.

The inchoative or conative imperfects, whose force is too seldom realized in the *RSV*, sometimes, though not always, fare better in the *NEB*: 'John tried to dissuade him' (Mt 3^{14}); 'he began to address them' (Mt 5^2, but what is wrong with 'teach'?); 'we tried to stop him' (Mk 9^{38}; but the force of the present imperative is missed in Jesus's reply, verse 39); 'he began to speak' (Lk 1^{64}, why not also in Mk 7^{35}?); 'their nets began to split' (Lk 5^6); 'they . . . began to discuss' (Lk 6^{11}); 'they began to ship water' (Lk 8^{23}). But the force of these imperfects is again lost in such instances as Mk 15^{23}; Acts 11^2, 13^5.

The durative significance of present imperatives of injunction is caught on many occasions (but not always; cf. Mk 9^{39}, already referred to). Thus we find: 'put away anxious thoughts' (Mt 6^{25}); 'weep no more' (Lk 7^{13}, 8^{52}, but why not also in Rev 5^5?); 'be unbelieving no longer' (Jn 20^{27}); 'sin must no longer reign' (Rom 6^{12};

G

but the 'must' is dubious). The distinction between the present and aorist imperative is well brought out in Romans 6[13]: 'you must no longer put . . . No: put . . .'. And the present and aorist infinitives of Jude verse 3 are also well translated: 'I was fully engaged in writing . . . when it became urgently necessary to write at once . . .'. On the other hand, the durative significance of present imperatives is not allowed in such passages as Matthew 6[19], 7[1], 10[31], Lk 11[7], John 5[45]. The translation of the aorist imperative and the pronoun in Matthew 26[39]—'let this cup pass me by'—creates a peculiar picture in the mind; and the phrase 'pass me by' occurs also in verse 42, where the poorly attested Koine text has apparently been adopted. The present and aorist imperatives in John 11[34] are still not differentiated; the translation remains, 'Come and see'.

The durative implication of the present participle in Galatians 5[8] was missed in the *RSV* where the translation is misleading on two counts: the 'him' in the *RSV* could be Paul, which it is not; and the durative force of the Greek participle is lost in the English 'called'. The *NEB* clearly and correctly represents Paul's Greek: '. . . it did not come from God who is calling you.' The rendering of the present participle at Luke 9[62] is also excellent: 'and then keeps looking back'; so is the translation of the aorist participle 'learned' in Acts 9[30] (*RSV*, 'knew'). We are, nevertheless, let down again by the translation of the present participle in Matthew 20[20] by 'begged'; and the effective force of the aorist participle in Matthew 26[10] is missed by being translated again (as in *RSV*) 'aware'.

Perfective (intensive) compound verbs are allowed their full meaning in some passages where they are under-translated in the *RSV*: 'searched him out' (Mk 1[36]; *RSV* 'followed him'); 'gulp down' (Mt 23[24]; *RSV* 'swallow'); 'joined issue with' (Acts 17[18]); (*RSV* 'met'). In other passages, however, the perfective force of these verbs is not brought out, as in the following cases: 'he will give' (Mt 16[27]; *RSV*'s 'he will repay' is better); $\dot{\alpha}\pi\acute{\epsilon}\chi\omega$ in Matthew 6[2, 5, 16], Luke 6[24], $\delta\iota\alpha\kappa\alpha\theta\alpha\rho\acute{\iota}\zeta\omega$ in Matthew 3[12]. The perfective significance of $\kappa\alpha\tau\alpha\kappa\alpha\acute{\iota}\omega$ is never captured; it is always translated like $\kappa\alpha\acute{\iota}\omega$; $\kappa\alpha\tau\alpha\mu\acute{\alpha}\theta\epsilon\tau\epsilon$ (Mt 6[28]) is still weakly translated 'consider'; the translation 'work out' (Phil 2[12]) does not do justice to the full import of the verb, no matter how familiar the English may be in this passage; and 'remove' (Heb 10[11]) is not quite adequate for $\pi\epsilon\rho\iota\alpha\iota\rho\acute{\epsilon}\omega$.

Whether a neuter is a generalizing neuter to indicate people is sometimes difficult to determine, but the one in 1 John 5⁴ probably is (although the *RSV* translators did not think so). The *NEB* renders, 'every child of God' (as against the *RSV*, 'whatever is born of God').

(3) The Meaning of Words

Many other words and phrases could be singled out as illustrations of just the right English translation, and they are all the more welcome in cases where the *RSV* is inadequate or misleading. Once again, there is space for just a few examples.

In Matthew 15¹⁷ (and Mk 7¹⁹) ἀφεδρών (which the *RSV* does not translate at all) is 'drain'; and Matthew's ἐκβάλλεται (which the *RSV* translates 'passes on', as though Matthew's verb were the same as Mark's) is 'discharged'. The Greek εὐρύχωρος of Matthew 7¹³ is 'plenty of room' (the *RSV* 'easy' is incorrect); καλῶς (Mk 7⁶) is 'right' ('Isaiah was right'). Ephesians 4¹³ has 'full stature of Christ'; σχιζόμενος in Mark 1¹⁰ is 'torn open', which translation recognizes the distinction (not reflected in the *RSV*) between Mark's verb and the *different* verb used in the parallels of Matthew and Luke. The difference between Luke's ἀρτυθήσεται (14³⁴) and Matthew's ἀλισθήσεται (5¹³) is correctly brought out (while the *RSV* misleadingly translates the two passages identically). 'Are you as dull as the rest?' (Mk 7¹⁸; cf. Mt 15¹⁶, Lk 24²⁵), and 'began to assail him fiercely' (Lk 11⁵³) are far better translations than their tamer *RSV* counterparts.

The translation of both πτῶμα (Mt 24²⁸) and σῶμα (in the parallel of Lk 17³⁷) as 'corpse' is better than the *RSV* translation of both words as 'body'; and ἀετοί is well translated 'vultures' rather than 'eagles' as in the *RSV*, where the whole saying remains unnecessarily enigmatic. Σὰρξ μία is once again rendered 'one flesh' (rather than just 'one': Mt 19⁵⁻⁶, Mk 10⁸); ἀπολῦσαι (Mk 10⁴) is sensibly translated 'divorce' (where the *RSV–KJV* 'put away' sounds too much like hiding in a closet); and χωρίζω (Mk 10⁹) is given its modern English equivalent 'separate' (rather than the somewhat obsolete *RSV–KJV* 'put asunder'). But σκληροκαρδία in this passage (Mk 10⁵) is not adequately translated by 'unteachable'.

In the *RSV* of Acts 8²⁷, 'Candace' appears to be the proper name of the queen (or, at least, may be so taken). The *NEB* correctly renders the meaning of the text by 'a high official of the Kandake, or Queen, of Ethiopia, in charge of all her treasure'. The translation at Acts 21[37]—'So you speak Greek, do you?'—is very good. So also the meaning of Luke 24[5] is rightly represented: 'Why search among the dead for one who lives?' (*RSV*'s 'the living', from *KJV* and Tyndale, is poor because the reference is not to 'the living' but to 'the living *one*', Jesus.)

We may rejoice that the British translators have not seen fit to add 'bread' to the text of Mark 14[20]. Unhappily, 'bread' was inserted here in the *RSV*, apparently via Goodspeed; but regardless of its source, it does not belong. To discover the nature of Jesus's Last Supper is difficult enough without translators confounding the issue by having Jesus dip 'bread' in verse 20 before he 'took bread' in verse 22. Finally, Paul's word play on ψυχή—ψυχικός in 1 Cor 15[44-6] is ingeniously represented in the English by a slight re-ordering of the Greek. Following the lead of the Vulgate, the *NEB* translates the adjective ψυχικός as 'animal', and the noun ψυχή with ζῶσαν as 'animate being', the word play being on *animate—animal*.

(c) *Consistency*

How consistent should a translator be in the English words he chooses to represent the Greek? The question is not easily answered. Bishop Lightfoot advocated regularly translating the same Greek word by the same English word; Jowett objected that this was 'a mistaken attempt at precision'. But one can err on either side. It is clearly a mistake always to translate the same Greek by the same English, for Greek words often had several meanings and were used in different senses. The RV-*ASV* erred on this side. On the other hand, if, for example, Jesus says the same thing (according to the Greek text) in Matthew, Mark and Luke, this identity should be apparent in the English translation. (By the same token, a variation in the Greek of one Gospel should be represented in the English).

But there are other situations in which inconsistency in translation is just as questionable. It is doubtful, for example, that a word occurring more than once in the same context and with the same meaning should be translated by different English words, with slightly different connotations, just for the sake of variety. It is doubtful that variety is preferable to accuracy. Potential error in exposition far outweighs possible gain in style; and while the translation should be good English, it should also translate the original as accurately as possible. Whether by oversight or intent, the *NEB* appears to err on the side of inconsistency. There follow a few examples of the translation of parallel passages in the Synoptic Gospels.

In Matthew 5[25-6], Luke 12[57ff], the same Greek words are translated differently, and different Greek words are translated identically. The same Greek is translated in Matthew 'once you are there you will not be let out', and in Luke 'you will not come out'. But two different words are both translated 'constable', and two other different words are both translated 'farthing' (unless the translators were following the unlikely D reading of Luke here).

In Matthew 8[10], Luke 7[9] ἐθαύμασεν is 'be astonished' (Mt) and 'admire' (Lk); and the same Greek is 'such faith' in Matthew and 'faith like this' in Luke. On the other hand, the distinction in Greek between the beginning of Matthew 7[1] and Luke 6[37] is lost in the *NEB* by being translated into the same English.

The Greek in Matthew 18[6], Mark 9[42], Luke 17[2] is identical (*RSV*, 'causes one of these little ones to sin'); but the *NEB* manages to translate it each time in a different way. The same verb in the doublet at Matthew 5[29], 18[9] is 'leads you astray' in the former, and 'is your undoing' in the latter. The translations at Matthew 27[33], Mark 15[22] agree—'Place of a skull'; but it is 'Place of the Skull' ('the' and capitals) at John 19[17]. The Greek ἠγέρθη is 'he has been raised again' in Matthew 28[6] (why 'again'?); but 'he has risen' in Mark 16[6], Luke 24[6].

Perhaps to make everyone happy the *NEB* translates υἱὸς Θεοῦ as 'a son of God' (Mk 15[39]), 'the Son of God' (Mt 14[33]), and 'Son of God' (minus the article, and in quotation marks, at Lk 1[35]). In Matthew 14[30] ἄνεμος is 'gale', but in verses 24 and 32 of the same narrative it is only 'wind'; ὁ πονηρός is 'the evil one' eleven times; but once, at Matthew 5[37], it is 'the devil'. What is there about this one passage that led to the different translation here? Ἁμαρτολοί are 'sinners' in Matthew 9[11, 13], but 'bad characters' in verse 10, Συντέλεια αἰῶνος is translated 'end of time' in Matthew 13[39-40 and 49], 28[20]; but 'end of the age' in Matthew 24[3], and 'climax of history' in Hebrews 9²⁶. The plural of fish is 'fishes' in Matthew 14¹⁷ and parallels, and Matthew 15³⁴ᶠᶠ and parallels. Why then is it just 'fish' in Mark 6⁴³?

The verb σκανδαλίζω is translated 'is a cause of stumbling' in Matthew 18⁶, but 'leads astray' in the parallel at Mark 9⁴². In fact, the *NEB* translates this verb in sixteen different ways, most expansively in John 16¹—'to guard you against the breakdown of your faith'.

In Matthew 15¹ the γραμματεῖς are 'lawyers', but 'doctors of the law' in the parallel of Mark 7¹. In Matthew 16²¹ (the second prediction of the Passion) they are 'lawyers', but in the parallels at Mark 8³¹ and Lk 9²² they are 'doctors of the law'. In the third prediction of the Passion they are 'doctors of the law' in Mark 10³³ and Matthew 20¹⁸. In Matthew 26⁵⁷, 27⁴¹ the γραμματεῖς are 'lawyers'; but in the parallels of Mark 14⁵³, 15³¹ they are 'doctors of the law'. In Matthew chapter 23 they are 'doctors of the law' in verse 2, just plain 'lawyers' in verse 13, and 'teachers' in verse 34!

The Greek εὐαγγελίζομαι is translated by a number of different verbs, but with 'Gospel' always capitalized; yet 'gospel' is written with a small g in Romans 15²⁰.

There are other passages in which different Greek is translated into the same English: Mark 5¹⁶, Luke 8³⁶, quite unalike in Greek, are identical in the *NEB* (with the exception of Mark's final phrase, omitted in Luke). The same participle in Matthew 9¹², Mark 2¹⁷ is translated 'the healthy'; but so also is a different participle in Luke's version (5³¹). Two differences between Mark 5¹⁹ and Luke 8³⁹ are ignored: different verbs translated 'tell', and different tenses of the same verb are translated 'has done'.

The over-inconsistency we have noted, something that is not particularly helpful or enlightening, but if anything, misleading, is not limited to the Synoptic Gospels. For example, ξύλον is rendered 'gallows' in 1 Peter 2²⁴, but 'gibbet' three times in Acts. The identical Greek is translated 'a stumbling-stone and a rock to trip them up' in Romans 9³³, and 'a stone to trip over, a rock to stumble against' in 1 Peter 2⁸. I fail to see any advantage, for the person who knows no Greek, in this kind of inconsistency.

NEB TRANSLATION OF A FEW KEY WORDS

We cannot take the space to discuss the regular translation of Χριστός as 'Messiah' in the Gospels and Acts, except in the few cases when Χριστός occurs with Ιησοῦς as a proper name, which is rendered 'Jesus Christ' or 'Christ Jesus': in Mark 1[1], John 1[17], 17[3], and twelve times in Acts. Of course in John 1[41], 4[25] Χριστός has to be rendered 'Christ' because 'Messiah' is the rendering of Μεσσίας in these verses. The author of the Fourth Gospel, who knew the word Μεσσίας, did not use it but used Χριστός; the *NEB* translators, however, preferred Μεσσίας. But the feeling persists that the Fourth Gospel should have been rendered in *John's* terms, and that this principle should also have been applied in the Synoptic Gospels and Acts.

The few exceptions to the practice of translating Χριστός as 'Messiah' in the Gospels should be mentioned. In Matthew 11[2], John 20[31] χριστός is rendered 'Christ'. In Luke 9[20] ὁ Χριστὸς τοῦ Θεοῦ is 'God's Messiah'; but in Luke 23[35] the same Greek is 'God's Anointed'.

Outside of the Gospels and Acts Χριστός is regularly rendered 'Christ' except in the following places: In Hebrews 11[26] ὁ Χριστός is quite misleadingly translated 'God's Anointed', as if the reference were simply to Moses. In 1 John 2[22], 5[1], and 2 John verse 9, where ὁ Χριστός is plainly a title the *NEB* renders 'the Christ', where one might expect 'the Messiah' (as in the Gospels and Acts); but in Romans 9[5] it is translated 'the Messiah'. Finally, ὁ Χριστός is 'Christianity' in Hebrews 6[1]; and 'Christian' in Romans 9[1], 16[7], 1 Corinthians 4[10], 7[22], 2 Corinthians 12[2, 19], 1 Thessalonians 4[16], 1 Peter 3[16].

The Greek δίκαιος, δικαιοσύνη, δικαιόω, etc., (righteous, righteousness, make righteous) are translated in many different ways. The proper English rendering is, as is well known, a very difficult matter, but variety of translation hardly solves the problem. The adjective is rendered in thirteen different ways. In three places (Mark 2[17] and parallels) it is 'virtuous', which I find most objectionable even in this passage; but in similar contexts (e.g. Luke 15[7]) it is 'righteous'. I am less enthusiastic about the translation of δίκαιος as 'good' or 'goodness' than were the translators who used these English words (combined) fourteen times (although never in Paul, *Pace*!).

The verb δικαιόω is only once translated with the word 'righteous' (in Lk 16¹⁵). In Luke 7²⁹ it is translated 'praised', but otherwise usually as 'justify', 'vindicate', or 'acquit'.

The noun δικαιοσύνη is also translated in numerous ways, among the more doubtful of which are the following: 'goodness' (Acts 13¹⁰; Rev 22¹¹, 2 Cor 5²¹—'the goodness of God himself'); or 'good' (2 Cor 11¹⁵; Tit 3⁵); 'religion' (Mt 6¹); 'morals' (Acts 24²⁵); 'benevolence' (2 Cor 9⁹⁻¹⁰); 'right living' (2 Tim 3¹⁶); and 'virtues' (1 Pet 3¹⁴).

These observations on the translation of this Greek root help to point up a moralistic tone that seems never very far away in the *NEB* as a whole. To illustrate this impression further, we may note that ὀργή is translated 'wrath' only once (Jn 3³⁶); but seventeen times as 'retribution', eight times as 'anger', and four times as 'vengeance', plus a few other translations. But is the 'ὀργή of God' in Paul, for instance, strictly and only God's *retribution*? The *NEB* translations of ὀργή have emotional and moralistic overtones which are much more pointed and explicit than they necessarily are in the Greek ὀργή or the English 'wrath'.

The translation of σάρξ (literally, 'flesh') is perhaps even more revealing:

Σάρξ is 'lower nature' in Rom 7⁵, 8³ᵃ, ⁴, ⁵, ⁶, ⁷, ¹²ᵃ, Gal 5¹³,¹⁶,¹⁷, ¹⁹, ²⁴, 6⁸, Col 2¹¹. Thus, apart from Christ, man 'lives on the level of his lower nature'. Σάρξ with ἁμαρτία is 'sinful nature' (Rom 8³ᵇ); οἱ ἐν σαρκὶ ὄντες (Rom 8⁸) is 'those who live on such a level'; and κατὰ σάρκα (Rom 8¹²ᵇ) is 'on that level' (i.e. on the level of the 'lower nature'). In Romans 7¹⁸, ²⁵ 'unspiritual nature' is substituted for 'lower nature'; and τῆς σαρκός (Col 2¹³) is translated 'morally'.

Thus we see that σάρξ is interpreted in moralistic terms, in terms of 'nature' and 'level of living'. It is made to connote weakness without including bondage. Σάρξ is interpreted as referring to level of living, and not also to a prior and more ultimate direction of living, to orientation.

Related to the translation of σάρξ is the translation of πνεῦμα (literally, 'spirit'). As ἐν σαρκί is 'on the lower level', so ἐν πνεύματι in Romans 8⁹ is 'on the spiritual level'. And in Romans 7⁶ we have 'the way of the spirit', by which is apparently meant the 'spiritual way'. Indeed, Romans 8[6b] is translated 'those who live on the level of the spirit (small s) have the *spiritual outlook*'. The frequent interpretation of 'flesh . . . spirit' in rather narrowly moralistic terms serves to illustrate a weakness in the *NEB* that is manifested in other contexts as well. Two examples are these: In Acts 19[21] it is said that 'Paul made up his mind' (with a footnote that the *Spirit* was involved). And in Romans 14[22-3] $\pi\iota\sigma\tau\iota\varsigma$ is translated 'conviction', Paul being represented as saying that 'anything which does not arise from conviction is sin'. Where is the response to God's grace in Christ? It is displaced by conviction.

THE IMPOSSIBILITY OF TRANSLATION

As the *NEB* Introduction affirms, translation remains an impossible art. In Romans 14[23] Paul says, literally, 'Everything that is not from $\pi\iota\sigma\tau\iota\varsigma$ is sin'. Now $\pi\iota\sigma\tau\iota\varsigma$ was used by Greek authors in many senses: faith, trust, reliability, confidence, oath, proof, pledge, etc. It is, of course, one of the key theological terms in Paul's letters, where it is usually translated 'faith' (also in the *NEB*). However, the British translators have apparently concluded that in Romans 14[22-3] $\pi\iota\sigma\tau\iota\varsigma$ does not have the theological significance it usually has in Paul, but that it is used there in a less theological sense, or in the more specific sense of 'conviction'. It is possible, of course, that the *NEB* is right in this translation, but it is at least equally possible (many would say it is probable) that the *NEB* is wrong. The point is that the translation 'conviction' considerably restricts Paul's meaning. It is far more precise than the apostle's Greek word, and, in addition, may not be his meaning at all. Translations tend increasingly to exclude possibilities of meaning that are allowed by the Greek text. The *NEB* is far more exact than the Greek, and clear when the Greek is ambiguous. A result is that in preaching and teaching from a translation, if the more precise English does not correspond exactly to the intention of the Greek, the more elaborately it is interpreted, the more erroneous the interpretation becomes. Where the Greek allows two or more meanings, the *NEB* selects one of the possibilities and thus excludes the alternatives. (Alternative translations in the footnotes, which appear in relatively few cases, do not solve the problem.)

No one should be under the illusion that the New Testament of the *NEB* can be used as a substitute for the Greek text. This was certainly not the intention of the translators. The *NEB* is not the equivalent, in English, of the original text; an English equivalent is simply not a possibility. The *NEB* is a kind of skeleton commentary, a commentary that lacks all elaboration. It attempts to interpret the Greek faithfully; but it must *interpret*. Following are a few illustrations (many more could be offered) of an exact English text with a restricted meaning, in cases where the Greek is open to at least one other interpretation.

'Our Master needs it' (Mk 11³ and parallels); 'It (the law) was added to make wrongdoing a *legal offence*' (Gal 3¹⁹); 'every sin to which we cling' (Heb 12¹); 'he was declared Son of God by a mighty act in that he rose from the dead' (Rom 1⁴); 'I received the privilege of a commission' (Rom 1⁵); 'The real light which enlightens every man was even then coming into the world' (Jn 1⁹—like *RSV*, but against Dodd); 'with God's right hand' (Acts 2³³, 5³¹); 'by his name' (Acts 4¹⁰); 'when you see all these things, you may know that *the end* is near (Mt 24³³, Mk 13²⁹); 'after singing *the Passover Hymn*' (Mt 26³⁰, Mk 14²⁶); 'unless a man has been born over again' (Jn 3³, with no footnote explaining the paronomasia); 'do you love me more than all else?' (Jn 21¹⁵); 'The words are yours' (Mk 15², Mt 27¹¹; and the English is the same in Mt 26²⁵, ⁶⁴, where the verb is not present but aorist). (One final, unrelated query: Why is Σίμων Πέτρος translated simply 'Peter' in Jn 18²⁵?)

Here, then, is a fresh translation of the New Testament. We welcome it! It has decided merit, and will unquestionably play a large and important role in the teaching and preaching of English-speaking Protestantism. Of the character and the extent of the significance it will have in the life and faith of the Church we cannot know now; but that it will be significant we need not doubt.

It seems to have been assumed in some quarters that the *RSV* is practically the equivalent (if not the exact equivalent) of the original Hebrew and Greek texts. The appearance of the *NEB*, whose English will be seen to be quite different from that of the *RSV* (not simply stylistically, but in meaning), will no doubt help to dispel this illusion. What a significant, if unintended, service the British translators will have performed for American Protestantism if the juxtaposition of the *NEB* with the *RSV* should reveal, like lightning from heaven, that *neither* translation can do, indeed, that *no* translation can do!

United Church Herald[1]

L. A. WEIGLE

...IN GENERAL, this is an excellent translation of its sort, consciously avoiding the structure and wording of the Tyndale–King James tradition. As an example of its quite new, striking renderings I quote 1 Corinthians 6[12]: '"I am free to do anything", you say. Yes, but not everything is for my good. No doubt I am free to do anything, but I for one will not let anything make free with me.' An admirably translated passage, too long to quote, is Luke 21[20-36].

On the other hand, the *Magnificat* (Lk 1[46-55]) is not well done. And the words of the Lord Jesus which Paul quotes (Acts 20[35]), 'It is more blessed to give than to receive' are changed into inferior English: 'Happiness lies more in giving than in receiving.'

I have a few major misgivings. The expression 'the Christ', which occurs forty-eight times in the Gospels and Acts has disappeared from these books except for one verse, John 20[31], and it is replaced in forty-five cases by 'the Messiah'. The result is that the reader of *NEB* gets no basis for understanding why the disciples should be called Christians (Acts 11[26]). No other English translation that I have seen replaces 'the Christ' by 'the Messiah' in this fashion, except C. C. Torrey, who was translating a hypothetical Aramaic text.

The *New English Bible* usually translates the word ἐκκλησία by 'congregation' when it is applied to a local group of Christians, and by 'church' when it is applied to the total body of Christian believers. It even translates ἐκκλησία by 'community' in 1 Corinthians 6[1, 4], 12[28], 14[4-5]; the last of these passages reads, 'help to build up the community'.

The word 'saints' which is used in the New Testament to designate the Christian believers, justified by faith in Christ, has been eliminated, being replaced in most cases by 'God's people'. The words 'sanctify' and 'sanctification' have also been eliminated.

[1] Vol. IV, No. 6 (23rd March, 1961), p. 30.

To discuss the issues involved in these substitutions of other terms for 'the Christ', 'the church', 'saints', and the related 'sanctify' and 'sanctification' lies beyond the limits set for this brief review.

The sound scholarship and the deliberate painstaking method that have shaped the *NEB* are beyond praise. I regret that we did not have the co-operation of a British Committee in the work upon the *Revised Standard Version*—the War prevented that. But there may be a good providence in the fact that we now have both a sound revision of the Tyndale–King James tradition and a new translation as competent as the *NEB*. The *Revised Standard Version* and the *New English Bible* will inevitably be competitive, but it may well be that in use they will mutually support one another.

Dunwoodie Review[1]

JAMES F. WELBY

...THE REVIEWER cannot find himself in agreement with the analysis of some who feel that the *NEB* is 'conciliatory—perhaps even condescending'. For them, it appears that the *NEB* is attempting to ease the conscience of unbelievers, as when 'If you wish to be perfect' (Mt 19²¹) is toned down to 'If you wish to go the whole way', and the children's 'angels' (Mt 18¹⁰) become 'guardian angels' (playing down the notion of angels ?). But such a criticism cannot be applied to these translations: 'To commit sin is to break God's law' (1 Jn 3⁴); 'This is his command: to give our allegiance to his Son Jesus Christ and love one another as he commanded' (1 Jn 3²³); 'Love the Lord your God with all your heart, with all your soul, with all your mind' (Mt 22³⁷). These are hardly conciliatory or condescending.

It is interesting to consider how the *NEB* treats points of disputed theological import. Some of these are worth our consideration. Since there is no doubt that Luke has taught the virgin birth of Christ (indeed, an important element in his account), it is not likely that the word $\pi\alpha\rho\theta\acute{\epsilon}\nu o\varsigma$ (which appears twice in Lk 1²⁷) should be translated as 'girl'.

Often enough, time elements are of considerable importance in the Bible. The *NEB*'s translation of $\mathring{\eta}\gamma\gamma\iota\kappa\epsilon\nu \mathring{\eta} \beta\alpha\sigma\iota\lambda\epsilon\acute{\iota}\alpha \tau o\hat{\upsilon} \Theta\epsilon o\hat{\upsilon}$ in Mark 1¹⁵ as 'the kingdom of God is upon you' seems to skirt the issue of whether the kingdom is imminent or actually present in the person of Jesus. From this translation, one cannot be sure where the *NEB* stands on the question, and the same may be said of its translation of the equivalent expression in Matthew 4¹⁷ and 10⁷. It is quite probable that in these texts partiality is being shown to the imminence idea. For in Luke 10⁹ that expression appears as 'the kingdom of God has come close to you', which points conclusively to the *NEB*'s preference for the notion of the imminence of the kingdom. It is likely that this notion was meant to be conveyed in

[1] Vol. II, No. 1 (January 1962), pp. 86–90.

Mark 1¹⁵ as well as Matthew 4¹⁷ and 10⁷. In the light of this, the translation of ἄρα ἔφθασεν ἐφ᾽ ὑμᾶς ἡ βασιλεία τοῦ Θεοῦ (Mt 12²⁸) as 'the kingdom of God has already come upon you' is probably to be taken as meaning simply that the coming of the kingdom is so vividly present to the mind of Jesus, that he speaks of it as something that has actually taken place. Other important time elements, such as those in Hebrews which point to the continuance of Christ's sacrifice, are properly evaluated in the *NEB*'s rendering of ἀναγκαῖον ἔχειν τι καὶ τοῦτον ὃ προσενέγκῃ (Heb 8³) as 'this one too must have something to offer', and in its translation of εὑράμενος (Heb 9¹³) as an aorist of coincidental action.

No unanimity has been reached on the translation of Romans 1⁴: τοῦ ὁρισθέντος υἱοῦ Θεοῦ ἐν δυνάμει, κατὰ πνεῦμα ἁγιωσύνης. In the *NEB* it appears as: 'But on the level of the spirit—the Holy Spirit—he was declared Son of God by a mighty act.' The fulcrum on which the whole verse turns in its grammatical construction is the *NEB*'s translation of "ὁρισθέντος" as 'declared'. Yet it seems that 'constituted' (or a like verb), with the grammatical structure called for by that translation, would more faithfully represent Paul's profound theology of the Resurrection, whereby the Son is made powerful (a power expressed in His communicating a share in His own life).

There are so many implications to St Paul's 'in Christ' and 'into Christ', that it is difficult to do justice to his meaning in every instance. The *NEB* often succeeds, but at times fails in this regard. Thus, 'we were baptized into union with Christ' (Rom 6³) is an interpretative translation that goes beyond the literal and gives a better sense to εἰς Χριστόν. Also, the *NEB*'s 'Christian men' (2 Cor 12¹⁹) is a more accurate rendering of "ἐν Χριστῷ" than Goodspeed's 'a follower of Christ'. But the *NEB*'s translation of Paul's "ἐν Χριστῷ" as 'the Christian dead' in 1 Thessalonians 4¹⁶ seems in this case to be too general and, therefore, a less precise expression of the Apostle's meaning. We find it better conveyed in Goodspeed's 'those who died in union with Christ'.

The translation of καὶ πάντες ἓν Πνεῦμα ἐποτίσθημεν (1 Cor 12¹³) as '. . . and that one Holy Spirit was poured out for all of us to drink' suggests that, like Cerfaux, the *NEB* sees a reference here to the Eucharist. Yet, earlier in 1 Corinthians 10³ ᵃⁿᵈ ⁴, the rendering of πνευματικός as 'supernatural' does not bring out the Eucharistic typology of the passage as clearly as 'spiritual' would have done. For it seems that the principal reason why Paul calls the food and drink of Israel πνευματικός is that he is here presenting them as types of the sacrament in which the Christ who became life-giving Spirit (1 Cor 15[45]) becomes the food and drink of the Christians. . . .

Sunday Telegraph[1]

T. S. ELIOT

THERE ARE three points of view from which any translation of the Bible may be examined: that of doctrine, that of accuracy of translation, and that of English prose style. In what follows I am concerned only with the question of style.

The translation of the Bible undertaken over 350 years ago at the suggestion of King James I was made by the best scholars in the kingdom. It was a revision of previous translations; the task was parcelled out between six committees, and a general committee spent over two years in revising the work of the six.

In the preparation of the *New English Bible*, of which only the New Testament has been completed and published, an equally careful procedure has been followed. There have been four 'panels', of which one has been responsible for the New Testament, and another is responsible for 'the literary revision of the whole'.

Again, the committees have been enlisted from among the best scholars in the kingdom, and, this time, with complete freedom of choice; for denominational considerations have played no part.

ERRORS OF TASTE

The age covered by the reigns of Elizabeth I and James I was richer in writers of genius than is our own, and we should not expect a translation made in our time to be a masterpiece of our literature or, as was the Authorized Version of 1611, an exemplar of English prose for successive generations of writers.

We are, however, entitled to expect from a panel chosen from among the most distinguished scholars of our day at least a work of dignified mediocrity. When we find that we are offered something far below that modest level, something which astonishes in its combination of the vulgar, the trivial, and the pedantic, we ask in alarm: 'What is happening to the English language?'

I shall give a few quotations in illustration, before examining

[1] No. 98 (16th December 1962), p. 7.

the principles of translation adopted by the translators, as set forth in the Introduction: principles which seem to me to take us some way towards understanding the frequent errors of taste in the translation itself.

The translation of a passage may be subjected to criticism on several grounds. I can illustrate this very well by examining a sentence in St Matthew (hereinafter referred to as 'Matthew', in conformity with the *New English Bible*) the earlier version of which will be a familiar quotation to many even of those who are ignorant of the Scriptures: 'Do not feed your pearls to pigs.'

We notice, first, the substitution of 'pigs' for 'swine.' The Complete Oxford Dictionary says that 'swine' is now 'literary' but does not say that it is 'obsolete'. I presume, therefore, that in substituting 'pigs' for 'swine' the translators were trying to choose a word nearer to common speech, even if at the sacrifice of dignity.

I should have thought, however, that the word 'swine' would be understood, not only by countryfolk who may have heard of 'swine fever', but even by the urban public, since it is still applied, I believe, to human beings as a term of abuse.

Next, I should have thought that the sentence would be more in accordance with English usage if the direct and indirect objects were transposed, thus: 'Do not feed pigs upon your pearls.' To make 'pearls' the direct object is, if I am not mistaken, an Americanism, and my belief is confirmed, rather than dispelled, by the examples of this usage given in the *Oxford English Dictionary*.

The most unfortunate result, however, is that the substitution of 'feed' for 'cast' makes the figure of speech ludicrous. There is all the difference in the world between saying that pigs do not *appreciate* the value of pearls, and saying, what the youngest and the most illiterate among us know, that they cannot be *nourished* on pearls.

TOO LITERAL

This is not the only instance in which a figure of speech, or illustration, has been ruined; though in some other places rather by literalness, as 'no man can be slave to two masters', which ceases to carry any admonition, and becomes merely a flat statement about the condition of slavery.

'Or how can you say to your brother, "Let me take the speck out of your eye", when all the time there is that plank in your own ?'

H

may be literally accurate but will certainly, if it is read in church, raise a giggle among the choirboys. As for the house built upon sand, 'down it fell with a great crash!'.

As for clarity, I find some passages more puzzling in the *New English Bible* than in the Authorized Version. Surely others besides myself will take no comfort from being told, as the first beatitude: 'How blest are those who know that they are poor.' (The translator of Luke is more nearly in accord with the Authorized Version here.)

And the unlearned, on being told that 'a man who divorces his wife must give her a note of dismissal', will marvel at the apparent facility with which the Hebrews could get rid of their wives. 'Bill of divorcement', even though it gives no clear notion of the process required by Jewish law, at least sounds ceremonious.

The foregoing examples are all taken from 'the Gospel according to Matthew', an Evangelist who seems to have been especially unlucky in his translator. The other Gospels, however, conform to the same style (or absence of style) in their monotonous inferiority of phrasing.

I wish nevertheless to quote one brief passage in order to give the translator of 'Luke' his due (Lk 3$^{14-15}$). To the soldiers who ask what they should do John the Baptist replies: 'No bullying; no blackmail; make do with your pay!'

I admit gladly that lapses of taste are less offensive when committed against a 'Letter'—that is to say, against what we have known heretofore as an 'Epistle'—than when committed against a Gospel. And there is much more justification, I will even say *need*, for modern translations of the Epistles than for modern translations of the Gospels.

A DIFFICULT WRITER

Some years ago Dr J. H. Oldham lent me the translation of St Paul's Epistles made by Gerald Warre Cornish (who fell in action, I believe, in the first World War). It struck me as admirable and very useful. To imagine, however, that a modern translation can make St Paul's meaning clear is an exaggeration: what it can make clear is what the familiarity of the Authorized Version may disguise from us—the fact that St Paul is a difficult writer.

A modern translation makes it easier for us to get to grips with the thought of St Paul: it does not relieve us of the necessity of using our own minds, any more than can a translation of Kant's *Critique of Pure Reason*.

And if the translations of Paul in the *New English Bible* did not offend our taste with Boeotian absurdities similar to those in the translations of the Gospels (e.g. Paul 'formulated the charge' that Jews and Greeks alike are all under the power of sin) they might take a respectable place among modern translations.

I do not propose to prolong my inventory of verbal infelicities in the *New English Bible*. *The Times Literary Supplement* of 24th March, 1961, had an excellent article on 'Language in the New Bible'; and the Trinitarian Bible Society has issued, as a leaflet, a useful list of specimens of bad taste, compiled by the Rev. Terence H. Brown and available at the price of one penny.

TRANSLATORS' AIMS

The instances I have given will suffice to prepare the way for an examination of the principles which the translators have set before themselves. These find their statement in the Introduction. I do not think that this Introduction has yet received enough attention.

According to the Introduction, the translators have set before themselves several aims: fidelity to what the author wrote; clarity; finer shades of idiom (than in the Authorized Version); to say in our own native idiom what they believed the author to be saying in his; and contemporaneity.

We are told that the language of the Authorized Version is 'even more definitely archaic, and less generally understood, than it was eighty years ago' (when the Revised Version was prepared) *'for the rate of change in English usage has accelerated'*.

I put this clause in italics, because it seems to me significant—and ominous. The English usage of eighty years ago, we are told, is out of date. And if the rate of change has accelerated, is it not likely to continue the acceleration? What is likely to be the fate of the *New English Bible* eighty years hence?

We are then told that for a version more modern than that of 1881 'an attempt should be made consistently to use the idiom of contemporary English to convey the meaning of the Greek'. This requirement of contemporaneity is emphasized at the end of the same paragraph: 'The present translators have been *enjoined* (italics mine) to replace Greek constructions and idioms by those of contemporary English.'

CHANGE FOR WORSE

No attempt is made to substantiate the assertion that the rate of change of English usage has accelerated, or to inform us in what respects English usage is changing. It does not seem to have occurred to the mind of the anonymous author of this Introduction that change can sometimes be for the worse, and that it is as much our business to attempt to arrest deterioration and combat corruption of our language, as to accept change.

Nor are we given any definition of 'contemporaneity'. Is it to be found in the writing of the best contemporary writers of English prose, and if so, who are they and who is to decide who they are? Or is it to be found in colloquial speech, and if so at what level of literacy?

Will the readers who find 'sweated all day in the blazing sun' suits them better than 'borne the burden and heat of the day' be the same as those who find 'extirpate' more 'contemporary' than 'destroy'?

When we turn to the description on the jacket we find that the aim was 'to be in style neither traditional nor modernistic'. If style is to be contemporary without being modernistic, the words 'contemporary' and 'modernistic' should be carefully defined.

FOR WHOSE USE?

At the time when the *New English Bible* was published, it seems that Dr Dodd appeared in a television programme and explained the purposes for which it was designed. As I did not hear him on that occasion, I quote from the article in *The Times Literary Supplement* to which I referred earlier:

In a helpful television programme . . . Dr Dodd, the director of the enterprise, told viewers whom the new Bible was intended for: it was, he said, for people who do not go to church, for a rising generation less well educated than formerly in classical and literary traditions, and for churchgoers so well accustomed to the language of the Authorized Version that they may have come to find it soothing rather than meaningful.

So long as the *New English Bible* was used only for private reading, it would be merely a symptom of the decay of the English language in the middle of the twentieth century. But the more it is adopted for religious services the more it will become an active agent of decadence.

There may be Ministers of the Gospel who do not realize that the music of the phrase, of the paragraph, of the period is an essential constituent of good English prose, and who fail to understand that the life of a reading of Gospel and Epistle in the liturgy is in this music of the spoken word.

The first appearance of the *New English Bible* in churches has, I believe, been in the reading of the Epistle for the day. Nothing will be gained, for the new version will be just as hard to grasp, when read in church, as the Authorized Version, and it will lack the verbal beauty of the Authorized Version.

To understand any version we must study it at home, or under direction. And if use of the *New English Bible* 'Letters' in churches is followed by adoption of the *New English Bible* Gospels, must we not look forward to the day when the Collects of Cranmer are revised for use in Anglican churches, to make them conform to 'contemporary English'?

It is good that those who aspire to write good English prose or verse should be prepared by the study of Greek and Latin. It would also be good if those who have authority to translate a dead language could show understanding and appreciation of their own.

Durham University Journal[1]

CHARLES GARTON

...IT IS, however, in this very field of style, that the new work has been most searchingly oppugned. The onslaught tends to come from such people as professors of English, and the gravamen of it is this. The Authorized Version, partly through the genius of its translators and partly because it came from the religious soul of a biblically committed people, achieved something in the history of the English language and in our whole culture which cannot now be repeated or remoulded, but only spoiled. It found out the uniquely appropriate treatment for its subject-matter, and it set standards of tone and rhythm which have engrained themselves in our race and inspired some of our greatest writers. Relatively to it, they argue, the new Bible *is* restyled and deplorably so, and they compare, especially, rhythm with rhythm to show how the glory has vanished and something banal and awkward been put in its place.[2] From here the attack broadens. Appropriate religious language, it is said, has, whether we are believers or not, an importance of its own at the cardinal moments and ceremonies of our lives. The impact of this book seems to defeat its own object. By losing atmosphere and truth of feeling, it loses essence, and so willy-nilly does a disservice to religion.

I wonder what, as coevals of Hieronymus, they would have had to say about the rhythms of the Vulgate. To reflect on that, or any similar moment in the long history of scripture, serves to throw into relief several things which they are taking for granted but which are very much open to question. They make the English Bible their absolute starting-point. On the literary level, they see it as a law to itself, and are not interested in the nature of its responsibility to the Hebrew and Greek originals. Besides, they look at it in isolation from other strands in the skein of English prose, such as

---

[1] Vol. LV, No. 1 (N.S. XXIV. 1), (December 1962), pp. 23–31.
[2] See the searching review by H. Gifford in *Essays in Criticisim*, Vol. XI (October 1961), pp. 466–70.

Hooker and the Prayer Book, as if the 1611 translators somehow had a patent of the rhythms of high seriousness. In showing its influence on later prose, they limit themselves to what is good and never ask whether there is a debit side to the account. Liturgically, they assume that religious language, to be appropriate, must be of this Jacobean texture. Agnostics develop particular passion on this last point, and spiritedly defend religion against the innovations of the religious. In all these ways the view that I am discussing seems to be too narrowly based and to be applying, in the literary sphere, a pontifical rigour of judgement which in the field of belief its partisans would not for a moment tolerate.

Now if we come down to brass tacks and look at the argument in its own terms, it does, up to a point, strike home. In certain comparisons of style, tone and rhythm, the new Bible, like the whole idiom to which it belongs, falls flat or comes off second-best. What is more, it does not even belong wholeheartedly to that idiom, but is sometimes reduced to inserting bits of old-fashioned religious jargon with incongruous effect. Under the first head, every reader will make his own selection of ichabod-passages. 'The low estate' or, as Coverdale had it, 'lowliness of his handmaiden', a phrase which haunts the mind even of the undevout, is replaced by 'so tenderly has he looked upon his servant, humble as she is', 'Image and superscription' becomes 'whose head is this, and whose inscription ?' and 'render unto Caesar', where the miraculous verb 'render' somehow gathers up the power of the whole story, is clipped down to a mere 'pay Caesar'. 'In the world ye shall have tribulation' is de-rhythmized into 'in the world you will have trouble', and 'my grace is sufficient for thee', which many a soul despairing of innocence or sanity must have clung to as a lifeline, has become 'my grace is all you need'. As to heterogeneity and the inweaving of archaism, that too is not far to seek. The translators say they have constantly tried to render the Greek into present-day English, 'that is, into the natural vocabulary, constructions, and rhythms of contemporary speech'. But the problem is ineluctable: what is natural modern English when you are addressing God or devils ? In using 'thou' for addressing God they have taken the right course: to have used it for God and men alike, as Knox does, would (no matter how folk are said to speak in Yorkshire and Lancashire) have kept the language under a too artificial rein. But 'behold' and 'begone' will also both be found; the former, of

Christ, where, in St John's Gospel at any rate, 'ecce homo' was perhaps felt to hallow the usage; the latter, of devils, where anything less was probably inadequate for getting them into the herd of pigs. 'Hewed out a winepress' and 'yielded an hundredfold' are more questionable and as for 'convert the rebellious to the ways of the righteous' and 'faith was counted to him as righteousness', they are intrusive and unnecessary fossils.

So it is true that we have a medium which is not so obviously dignified and not so aurally satisfying as the old one, and a style which is not always at ease with itself; though it may be remarked here that the Authorized Version had parochialities and discomforts of its own and has exerted bad influence as well as good, such as that 'repetitive and throbbing and' which has been castigated in one of our modern poets. The nub of the question is, can twentieth-century pedestrian prose—not the semi-poetic prose of Lawrencian rhapsody—bear the weight of the biblical message in the compass of its own quieter rhythms? Can it adapt, as it were, to plain glass and sunlight what was formerly co-elemental with the arches and storied windows of the perpendicular nave? The answer is that it can if it cares enough.

> Love is patient; love is kind and envies no one. Love is never boastful, nor conceited, nor rude; never selfish, not quick to take offence. Love keeps no score of wrongs; does not gloat over other men's sins, but delights in the truth. There is nothing love cannot face; there is no limit to its faith, its hope, and its endurance.

Incongruities there are bound to be, because the Bible has much to say which does not come easily within the ambit of modern man's thinking at all. But language, if urgent and vital, as the new Bible for the most part is, can tolerate and even exploit these awkwardnesses, just as the Authorized Version tolerated and exploited 'strain at a gnat' and 'where neither moth nor rust doth corrupt'. A style is not necessarily botched for being somewhat mixed, and neither those who attack nor those who defend the new Bible would have liked to see it dressed in an exclusive atticism. . . .

But how deep a mark the new translation will make depends only in part upon its literary quality. It depends also on two not easily reconcilable factors: upon what measure of authority it is felt to carry, and upon how plain and untrammelled is the voice in which it speaks to the Church and to the world. All who have learned the grammar of assent and are committed members of a Church desire to feel that the particular Bible they use has the confidence of their Church and the approval of those whom, spiritually and in the upbringing of their children, they most deeply trust. As the common labour of many churches, the new version will carry for most Christians in Britain the necessary measure of authority. For the world at large its greatest strength will lie in its faithfulness and self-reliance. That it is faithful at heart, anyone can find out by scrutiny and comparison. Its self-reliance rests on the fact that it is offered without exegetical notes or directives about interpretation, offered responsibly by believers, but frankly and without ties, to the widest generality of men.

To certain old antagonisms it may succeed in bringing a reconciling touch. Its clarity and rapidity, by dissuading men from tearing the individual text from its context, will abate some of the eccentricities of biblical sortilege and fundamentalism. It so clearly shows Paul distinguishing between what he has a divine commission to say and what he says of himself that it may well give pause to the more extravagant theories of inspiration. At the same time, by reminding us of how endemic from the very beginning was schism and strife, it will correct rash dreams of a Christian golden age in the past. By a self-denying restraint in the use of the word 'church', it begs as few questions of ecclesiology as possible. By vividly recalling to us how the early Church was organized, it helps Episcopalian and Presbyterian to understand each other. Consider the saying: 'for ye were as sheep going astray, but are now returned unto the Shepherd and Bishop of your souls.' As a piece of language, that verse from the old Bible surely ranks with the collect for Ash Wednesday as one of the most perfect sentences ever uttered in English. The new version substitutes 'Guardian' for 'Bishop', and an Anglican might jump to the suspicion that it was the nonconformists here who huffed and puffed till they blew the house down. But he has only to consult Knox on the same verse to see that this is not so. In spite of the Vulgate's *episcopum*, Knox likewise dropped 'Bishop'. The sanctity of the Latin and the sublimity of the English have both alike had to give way to what honest but fallible men hope is nearer the truth.

Western man being what he is, however, there are other old

antagonisms which may prove more deeply ingrained. The translators say that their handiwork 'is offered simply as the Bible to all who in reading, teaching, or in worship, may care to use it'. Picture an irenically-minded Roman Catholic taking them at their word. What then? He will read in St Paul:

Have I no right to take a Christian wife about with me, like the rest of the apostles . . ., and Cephas? (1 Cor 9[5]).

What is all this about the apostles and Cephas (i.e. St Peter, the first Pope) traipsing their wives round in the course of their priestly labours? The whole thing seems sadly undisciplined and he had better consult the Catholic version.

Nay, have we not the right to travel about with *a woman who is a sister*, as the other apostles do, . . . and Cephas?

Christian wife indeed! What audacious mendacity in the first rendering! What a brazen distortion by uxorious ministers! The one ground for hope lies in what may happen next. If such a reader looks into it sufficiently, he will come upon the surprising fact that, as far as the isolated words go, the Greek could have either meaning. This might set him considering imaginatively the whole context and eventually perhaps analysing the respective claims of authoritative guidance on the one hand and probability on the other. The type of thinking which this involves will be by no means wasted. . . .

Essays in Criticism[1]

HENRY GIFFORD

OVER THE past hundred years literature has been steadily losing ground; it no longer commands the centre, and has now given up a main citadel, the English Bible. Only yesterday the cadences of the Authorized Version controlled our speech, and provided a measure for high seriousness:

> He is the rock of defence for human nature; an upholder and preserver, carrying everywhere with him relationship and love. In spite of difference of soil and climate, of language and manners, of laws and customs: in spite of things silently gone out of mind, and things violently destroyed; the Poet binds together by passion and knowledge the vast empire of human society, as it is spread over the whole earth, and over all time.
>
> Anna's soul was put at peace between them. She looked from one to the other, and she saw them established to her safety, and she was free. She played between the pillar of fire and the pillar of cloud in confidence, having the assurance on her right hand and the assurance on her left. She was no longer called upon to uphold with her childish might the broken end of the arch. Her father and her mother now met to the span of the heavens, and she, the child, was free to play in the space beneath, between.

Passion and knowledge used that kind of utterance. It was a birth-right. Quite suddenly it has ceased to be; and the translators, turning to 'the current speech of our own time'—more stagnant than current—have shut themselves in a one-generation culture. The new rendering does not seek to replace the Authorized Version, but with a million copies already marketed, the effect will be to schedule the older Bible as an Ancient Monument (Open on Sundays 11-12 a.m. and 6.30-7.30 p.m. Keys with Vicar). The translators wrote largely for youth, for the man in the street, for

[1] Vol. XI (October 1961), pp. 466–70.

the victims of an illiterate Press and of television personalities
with a vocabulary of four hundred words. The English language is
becoming a dustbowl, the deposits of centuries blown away, and a
thin temporary soil remaining. Yet the Authorized Version could
still serve as a wind-break. Look now at the denuded scene.

It is principally a loss of rhythm, and thus of the passions and
sensibility that were expressed through that rhythm. Tyndale, who
moulded the character of the New Testament as we had previously
known it, thought and felt with the energy of rural Gloucester-
shire, and at its pace. This can be shown from the parable of the
tares (Mt 13). First, the new rendering:

> When the corn sprouted and began to fill out, the darnel could
> be seen among it. The farmer's men went to their master and
> said, 'Sir, was it not good seed that you sowed in your field?
> Then where has the darnel come from?' 'This is an enemy's
> doing,' he replied. 'Well then,' they said, 'shall we go and gather
> the darnel?' 'No,' he answered; 'in gathering it you might pull
> up the wheat at the same time.'

In the Authorized Version it goes:

> So the servants of the householder came and said unto him, Sir,
> didst thou not sow good seed in thy field? from whence then
> hath it tares?
> He said unto them, An enemy hath done this. The servants
> said unto him, Wilt thou then that we go and gather them up?
> But he said, Nay; lest while ye gather up the tares, ye root up
> also the wheat with them.

It gains immeasurably through the pauses. After the servant's
question, the householder seems to think before answering: the
reader can feel the weight of what has happened. Again there is a
pause indicated before the servants put their next question. The
new rendering, 'Well then' they said, 'shall we go and gather the
darnel?' doesn't allow for the slow processes of rural rumination.
And the master has no authority, if they can speak to him like that.

The insensibility to rhythm and so to the dramatic tempo of a
scene can betray itself in the botching of a single word. Tyndale's
account of Christ stilling the tempest (Mt 8) has:

Then he arose/and rebuked the wynds and the see/and there folowed a greate calme.

The Authorized Version improves by putting *was* for *followed* (*was*, the 'fact presented in the most naked simplicity possible', as Wordsworth explained a similar use in 'Resolution and Independence'). The new translators (advised, no doubt, by that amateur yachtsman who is said to have been called in for St Paul's shipwreck) make it 'a dead calm', and so kill the wonder.

It may be that Tyndale and King James's men (like Rembrandt, in his painting of New Testament scenes) contributed their own solemn chiaroscuro. The present translators have had the benefit of innumerable scraps of papyrus uncovered in the Egyptian sands and are perhaps right to recognize the Greek as more 'flexible and easy-going'. St Paul in the Authorized Version is an impressive though difficult writer (a Carlyle with literary sense). 'Be not deceived; God is not mocked . . .' Today he rattles this out on the keys of his typewriter: 'Make no mistake about this: God is not to be fooled . . .' 'Go to now, ye rich men, weep and howl for your miseries that shall come upon you.' 'Next a word to you who have great possessions. Weep and wail over the miserable fate descending on you.' The Apostle was a busy man, clearly; and like other busy men he is driven to use clichés. 'Weep and howl' has the force of medieval wall-painting; 'Weep and wail' is the language of sedentary men who have lost the capacity to see and touch. 'Are not two sparrows sold for a farthing?' Christ asks in the Authorized Version (which follows Tyndale). 'Are not sparrows two a penny?' is wrong, because 'two a penny' is a cliché; like the pennies that drop, and are offered for thoughts, the coin has no existence. But 'two sparrows for a farthing' implies real birds and real money. They must have been cheap food, and today small birds are still eaten in Mediterranean countries.

Translators are perhaps bound to mediate the world of their own time. Here we can recognize the grey, anonymous, oatmeal-paper forms, the ill-phrased regulations, the barren communiqués and reassuring statements from which there is no escape this side of the grave—and not on the other side if the *New English Bible* is to be trusted. This is a world where 'decrees are issued for a general registration'; where 'a pupil is not superior to his teacher, but everyone, when his training is complete, will reach his teacher's level' (see Ministry of Education circular, 'Notes towards the definition of postgraduate levels'); where the 'existing authorities', having been 'instituted', proceed to 'devote their energies'; where people 'meet in conference to plan' an unspeakable crime; and where the Christians at Ephesus 'give rise to a serious disturbance', when the silversmiths, at a meeting with 'workers in allied trades', conclude that if this goes on, their 'line of business will be discredited', and so good-bye to their 'high standard of living'. In this world women have 'elaborate hair-styles'; 'the glitter and the glamour are lost, never to be yours again'; obligations are imposed, moments are critical, rations are issued at the proper time, and 'the worldly are more astute than the other-worldly in dealing with their own kind'.

In this world St Peter escapes from prison, or rather is 'rescued from Herod's clutches' (Acts 12):

All at once an angel of the Lord stood there, and the cell was ablaze with light. He tapped Peter on the shoulder and woke him. 'Quick! Get up', he said, and the chains fell away from his wrists. The angel then said to him, 'Do up your belt and put your shoes on'. He did so. 'Now wrap your cloak round you and follow me.' He followed him out, with no idea that the angel's intervention was real. . . .

It is an exciting narrative; there were a thousand such escapes in the war; if Peter read our newspapers, of course he would have 'no idea' that an angel was helping him. But the cell ablaze with light hasn't (for me) any mystery: someone must have switched on the supply at the mains.

Thus ultimately the tone is at fault. The translators, as we know, submitted their English to a literary panel, dozing brothers of the craft who had neither ears to hear nor eyes to notice the countless infelicities, the substitution on every page of lax, uncompelling speech for what should be direct and vigorous: 'What is your opinion about the Messiah?' (not, 'What think ye of Christ?'). 'What action are we taking?' (not, 'What do we?'). The translators have never challenged their reader, never risked an unfamiliar concept or a remarkable word. Earnest and devoted men, they have damaged the Christian myth, so that the cruel paradox emerges: it is possible to believe and not wholly to understand; and some that do not believe can yet understand the essential poetry. They have done wrong to our language, by not stretching it at any point; the richest of all the world's languages, treated as post-office savings. And finally they have made things yet more difficult for the poet, by their tacit assumption that the marvellous can no longer find words of equivalent beauty to express it. 'From him that hath not shall be taken away even that which he hath.'

'Old Wine: New Bottles'[1]

MARTIN JARRETT-KERR, C.R.

Many of the habits of language in our culture are no longer fresh or creative responses to reality, but stylized gestures which the intellect still performs efficiently, but with a diminishing return of new insight and new feeling. Our words seem tired and shopworn. They are no longer charged with their original innocence or with the power of revelation. . . . We add to our technological vocabulary by joining together used scraps, like a reclaimer of old metals. We no longer fuse the raw materials of speech into new glory as did the compilers of the King James Bible. . . . Compare the grey jargon of the contemporary economist to the style of Montesquieu. Set the counting-house prose of the modern historian next to that of Gibbon, Macaulay, or Michelet. Where the modern scholar cites from a classic text, the quotation seems to burn a hole in his own drab page.[2]

If this is a true description of the condition of our time, as most literary critics would agree that it is, what can the contemporary translator do? Mr Henry Gifford, in the preceding article, says (in effect) that the only thing he can or should do is to shut up. Since the King James Bible is still in our midst, though no doubt treated with respect rather than with understanding, approached with the soft tread of the visitor stepping reverently up to the display of Ming vases, and since it is one of the few remaining preservatives of our language from decay, the translator should be paid off and his wages transferred to the curator.

There is a real problem here, and it will not do to dismiss it by saying that 'we've been here before'. The defenders of the *New English Bible* say this. They say, for instance, that St Augustine was just as embarrassed by the crude and inelegant style of Koine

---

[1] This article was written specially for this volume; it contains the substance of two shorter notices produced soon after the appearance of the translation.
[2] George Steiner, *The Death of Tragedy* (1961), p. 314.

Greek (the language of the New Testament) as our literary critics are by the flat prose of the *NEB*. This is perfectly true. And it is also true that the King James Bible itself, which we regard now as the yardstick, was not always accepted with the enthusiasm we accord it.

The late Bible . . . was sent to me to censure: which bred in me a sadness that will grieve me while I breathe, it is so ill done. Tell his Majesty that I had rather be rent in pieces with wild horses, than any such translation by my consent should be urged upon poor churches. . . . The new edition crosseth me. I require it to be burnt.'[3]

This was the scornful judgement upon what we now know as the Authorized Version by a Dr Hugh Broughton, 'a Hebrew and Greek scholar of great erudition and international repute in the seventeenth century'. But he was not invited to be one of the translators, and perhaps there is an element of personal pique in the criticism.

Thus criticisms of the *NEB*, on stylistic grounds, are met by saying, first that the prose of the King James Bible is not itself always impeccable: we have become so accustomed to regarding it as one of the supreme masterpieces of world literature that we do not often stop to notice how stuffed the language sometimes is, how frequently periphrases or the building up of long series of dependent clauses clog the advance of meaning. Second, it is sometimes hinted that perhaps the King James Bible was not so influential on the English language and literature as we have always assumed: and reference is made to Professor C. S. Lewis's brilliant Ethel M. Wood lecture on 'The Literary Impact of the Authorized Version'[4] in which he suggests that the notion of the AV's enormous influence upon our literature is a creation of, and therefore is limited to, the Romantic Movement. And finally it is suggested that some of the very characteristics for which the *NEB* is faulted are characteristics for which New Testament Greek was also faulted by the Christian Fathers brought up in a classical tradition. For instance, it has been stated that the word ἐπιούσιον in the Lord's Prayer is really a piece of 'office slang'—and therefore the

---

[3] I am indebted to Dr Glyn Simon, Lord Bishop of Llandaff, for this quotation.
[4] Reprinted in C. S. Lewis, *They Asked for a Paper* (Bles, 1962).

I

accusation that the *NEB* translators use 'the English of bureaucrats' is a tribute to the accuracy of their translation, rather than a condemnation of the poverty of their style. What shall we, then, say to these things?

I think we must start by admitting some justice in these statements. It is very likely that, as Bro. George Every, SSM, has suggested,[5] social conditions in our own time are very much more like those of New Testament times than those of Tudor times: and therefore to regard Tyndale or King James as the norm will be not merely archaism but disloyalty—disloyalty to the Lord of history. And Bro. George continues (he is speaking not of the *NEB* but of liturgical language today, and of the *NEB* only in so far as the new version is used in worship):

Rhetoric is very nearly a dead art, killed by the intimacy of wireless. . . . What we need in liturgy is not familiar conversation or rhetoric, but rhythmical response. I think this is possible, and it may come if . . . (those concerned with liturgical revision) can be weaned from their exclusive interest in the Primitive Church and will pay some attention to developments in those churches and countries where corporate worship in a common language persisted, and not only in the city where liturgy was dead at the start.

And he goes on to say that we need translations which will help to 'deflate the image of the biblical period', and to remind us that

the early Church started with a lot of small shopkeepers and traders, uprooted displaced persons in cosmopolitan towns, a most unsavoury lot of human materials, without much style and with a very untidy hotch-potch of ideas. The country men came in later. For anything that you can call a Christian culture you have to wait until the nations begin to be integrated into the faith. That is why the early Church provides an unsatisfactory model for theological thought and liturgical development, but we are drawn to it by real resemblances between our rootless condition and theirs. The same kind of people like . . . (modern translations like the *NEB*), who liked the apocryphal acts and the Clementine recognitions.

[5] In a personal communication to the author.

Bro. George suggests that those of us who are concerned to protect literary values now would have found the New Testament 'very hard to take'; and he points out that Tyndale himself didn't see a beautiful, homogeneous society with shared values and high literary standards:

What Tyndale rightly saw was decay. . . . Better Red Indians and Bushmen, whose culture is at least integrated. . . . We have never had a Christian culture here in the West. The most we can say is that we have sometimes come near it. It is the Gospel itself that makes achievement so difficult, and compels us in this world to make do with something less.

This view can be supported by the thesis of an art expert, who is, however, less pessimistic about the possibility of achieving a Christian culture. Professor Wladimir Weidle, in a little book published some years ago,[6] argued that before a new, developed Christian art was possible there had to be (or at any rate, there was) a prior movement of asceticism, of cultural puritanism. The art of the Catacombs, he says, eschews the graces of contemporary humanist expertise: the pictures are, especially when compared with the superb sculpture of the Greeks which still survived at that time, crude, badly drawn, but vigorous. On the other hand, the classical style had reached a point of exhaustion: it needed new life, new vigour, new convictions. This was what Christian 'primitivism' brought. It was only after this period of austerity that classical modes and conceptions could, much later, be safely incorporated into the now securely held Christian world-view. And M. Weidle calls this period of austerity 'The Baptism of Art' in the double sense, that baptism implies a descent into the purifying waters before the emergence into daylight; but also that the actual themes of 'Christian Art' at this early period were almost limited to illustrations of the rites of Initiation.

On this argument, the *NEB* could be defended as precisely a piece of necessary self-denial: a return to the catacombs. Just as (it will be said) the British Cathedrals no longer mean what they once meant—the public and corporate expression, in architecture and function, of the consecration of a religion-culture; so the Bible is no longer the book which can, in sonorous style, provide the

[6] Wladimir Weidle, *The Baptism of Art* (Dacre Press, 1951), *passim*.

(so to speak) prompt-copy for the staging of that religion-culture. Let Christians accept the situation: let them no longer try to impose a public image which has in fact faded or simply disappeared. Let the Bible in the AV be read as literature—there are plenty of heroic stories, especially in the Old Testament, which can be salvaged from the dustbin when the Bible as faith-centre is thrown out. But then let Christians have their own version of the Bible, as near to the crudities of the original as may be, a version which could (fortunately) never be read as literature, but which, in its stark, undecorated style will be able to steal into the hearts of those who are looking, not for literary exaltation or aesthetic fruition, but for a word of truth in an age of deceit.

Well: but *is* this what the translators who produced the *NEB* had in mind? When, for instance, we are told that the Greek word ἐπιούσιον in the Lord's Prayer is a bit of first-century 'commercialese', one might expect the *NEB* (if its aim were what some of its defenders say) to translate it into English commercialese ('Give us this day our allocation of bread for the current inst.' might perhaps do it). But in fact (in Mt 6¹¹ and Lk 11³) they retain the 'daily' of the AV. Is this because they did not have the courage of their convictions?

But it is not clear from their Introduction that their aim was a slavish recapturing of the mode of speech of Koine Greek. They were (they say) instructed to use 'the idioms of contemporary English'; their rendering was to be 'into the current speech of our time'; and so they have attempted to turn the Greek 'into the English of the present day, that is, into the natural vocabulary, constructions, and rhythms of contemporary English'. The word 'speech', and the emphasis upon 'rhythms', suggests that they had in mind *spoken* English (which can, of course, be rather different from written English); and there is no doubt that their hope was that the *NEB* would be read aloud at acts of worship and in church. If the project had been linked to a more general plea— 'back to the Catacombs' (or to their contemporary equivalent)— this surely would have had to be made much more clear than it was. Therefore one must assume that the translators' aim was a more modest one—the precise aim stated in their Introduction, and no more. But from another point of view it could be said that this aim was a more ambitious one: to try to do again, in contemporary English, what the AV tried to do in the English of the seventeenth century: even to try, by the employment of a contemporary style, to put the Bible back into the position it once held in English life and culture.

But whether the aim was modest or ambitious, it could not have been achieved without a fairly clear picture in the minds of the translators of what 'contemporary English' is. What in fact was that picture? For there are many kinds of contemporary English. There is this:

It may not be fanciful to look ahead to the time when a four-per-cent yield is the hallmark of a company with doubtful prospects. Such a tendency is, of course, a basic readjustment in market outlook which has nothing to do with short-term economic prospects; it is comparable to the major readjustment which took place when share prices rose to take account of assets growth once the Socialist shackles were finally struck off.[7]

Or this:

For the smaller industrial organization unable to justify the outright purchase of its own system, arrangements have been made with local waste-removal contractors to operate the equipment whereby a nominal charge is made for the hire of containers used for the on-site storage of waste together with a further charge for the pick-up and disposal of each container at agreed intervals.[8]

These may seem unfair choices, for they are taken from a brokers' report and a technical trade article. But this sort of language does manage to stain its way into ecclesiastical contexts:

At an early stage it became clear that it could not be assumed that the laity in the Church, and perhaps not always the clergy, had such a vital sense of the necessity and importance of cathedrals in the life of the Church that they would willingly face financial responsibilities and sacrifices in order to maintain them.[9]

[7] Manchester Brokers: quoted in *Investors Chronicle* (14th April 1961).
[8] *South Wales Spectator*, Vol. III, No. 24 (March 1962), p. 34.
[9] *Church Assembly Report*: cited in *The Times Literary Supplement* (9th March 1962), p. 161.

We must face the fact—which the translators do not seem to me to have faced—that ours is not a very happy time for producing a translation which could ever be a lasting treasure in the way that the Authorized Version has been. And unfortunately it seems as if it is precisely *religious* writing in our time that collects all the worst tricks, the weakest vocabulary and the flabbiest rhythms of contemporary prose. Sometimes this religious writing is bright, chatty and superficial, as in so much of the late Dorothy Sayers's radio sequence, *The Man Born to be King*:

> Listen. There was a man with two sons, and he told them to go and work on his allotment. And one of them said, cheerfully, 'Yes, rather, Dad'. But he met some friends and forgot all about it and never did a stroke. The other son said: 'No, I won't go. I hate digging'. But afterwards he thought, 'Oh well, I suppose I'd better', and went off grumbling, and did as he was told. Now which of these two did the will of his father? It doesn't need an answer, does it? . . .
>
> (Come) . . . We'll take a boat and go across the Lake to Bethsaida and spend the night in the mountains. And the Lord God of Israel shall give rest unto his people.[10]

Here we find Jesus talking, sometimes in the language of 'Mrs Dale's Diary', or of 'The Archers', and the next moment in the language of the AV.

Sometimes the language of religious writing is just soggy and dead, as in so many popular religious novels of our day. Here, from the best-selling novel, *The Silver Chalice*, is a description of St Peter:

> The hair and beard of the apostle were snow-white and most benevolently tended and curled. He was dressed in linen of a matching whiteness. But it was a change in his attitude that was most to be remarked. This was . . . a man who knew how to command, how to make his will accepted. The earnest-faced people who filled the room waited on his words.

And then Peter speaks, referring to the villain of the story, Simon Magus:

[10] Dorothy Sayers, *The Man Born to be King* (1943), pp. 147–8.

We have been too much concerned with this wicked man. He and his knavish tricks will soon cease to be of any consequence. ... Hearken to me still. ... The words I am going to say to you have been in my mind for a very long time. I give utterance to my thoughts now because I am sure the Lord is putting the words in my mouth so that ye may know His will.[11]

We can't help noticing the clichés: but also the uncertainty about what sort of 'period language' to use. Between one sentence and another St Peter switches arbitrarily from 'you' to 'ye'.

And yet there is prose of quite a different stamp being written in our time. Here is a passage from a contemporary novelist—though admittedly the novel was written a long time ago:

At that moment the carriage entered a little wood, which lay brown and sombre across the cultivated hill. The trees of the wood were small and leafless, but noticeable for this—that their stems stood in violets as rocks stand in the summer sea. There are such violets in England, but not so many. Nor are there many in Art, for no painter has the courage. ... Philip paid no attention at the time: he was thinking what to say next. But his eyes had registered the beauty, and next March he did not forget that the road to Monteriano must traverse innumerable flowers.[12]

Or, if that should seem a little too quiet and smooth for the fierce vigour of the Bible, here is a quite different sample from an impetuous, overwhelming writer whose prose, like his poetry, is undisciplined perhaps, but as exciting and lethal as a jungle:

I've just come back from three dark days in London, city of the restless dead. It really is an insane city, and filled me with terror. Every pavement drills through your soles to your scalp, and out pops a lamp-post covered with hair. I'm not going to London again for years; its intelligentsia is so hurried in the head that nothing stays there; its glamour smells of goat; there's no difference between good and bad.[13]

[11] Thomas B. Costain, *The Silver Chalice* (1953), pp. 459–62.
[12] E. M. Forster, *Where Angels Fear to Tread* (1905), p. 30.
[13] Dylan Thomas, *Letters to Vernon Watkins* (1957), p. 49. (Letter of 20th December 1938.)

The real problem for a translator today is the almost un-plottable area over which contemporary prose tends to sprawl: what is he to take as his model, when the samples range as widely as the examples I have quoted? The translators of the *NEB* had in their team three literary 'experts', to whom the drafts were submitted.[14] But prose is not something that can be 'tidied up'; and this is only one example of the more inclusive difficulty that a Committee is not the ideal author of any literary work. (It is sometimes retorted that the AV was the work of a Committee: but it was the work of a Committee not making a translation from scratch, but revising the work of one author—Tyndale.) And in any case, however 'expert' the literary 'experts', the dice were loaded against them. To show what I mean: here are two passages of seventeenth-century prose, written within about thirty years of each other. Their subject-matter is almost as disparate as the passages from the *Investors Chronicle* and Mr E. M. Forster, quoted above: but the language in which they are written belongs to the same family, and how good the family is!

The first is a sophisticated passage from Sir Walter Raleigh's *History of the World* (written in 1603, while he was in the Tower, awaiting execution). He is speaking of Death:

He takes account of the rich, and proves him a beggar; a naked beggar, which hath interest in nothing, but in the gravel that fills his mouth. He holds a glass before the eye of the most beautiful, and makes them see therein their deformity and rottenness; and they acknowledge it. O eloquent, just and mighty death! whom none could advise, thou hast persuaded; what none hath dared thou hast done; and whom all the world hath flattered, thou only hast cast out of the world and despised: thou hast drawn together all the far-stretched greatness, all the pride, cruelty and ambition of man, and covered it all over with these two narrow words, *Hic jacet*.

The other passage is from a popular Elizabethan novel, *Long Meg of Westminster*, about a tough, young woman from Lancashire who on her Amazonian travels was prepared to take on all comers. In this passage she meets some thieves, and her companions are scared. But Meg stands firm.

14 This is not quite accurate; see Introduction, p. xi. (Ed.)

One of the thieves with a good sword and buckler stepped before and said, Stand. Stand? quoth Meg, what mean you by that? Marry, quoth he, Gentlemen, 'tis hot weather, and you must go lighter home by your gowns and your purses. . . . Nay, you cowardly knave, quoth she . . . I must have a hundred marks out of your flesh; you are two to one, lay me down the hundred marks to our gowns and purses, and they that win all, wear all, I or you.

Content, quoth the thieves, and because thou art so lusty, when we have well beswinged thee, we'll turn thee out of thy smock, and let thee go home naked. Do your worst, quoth she: now lasses, pray for me. With that she buckled with these two sturdy knaves, and hurt the one sore, and beat down the other, that they entreate her upon their knees to spare their lives.

Can you find a 'green-back' today which is written in such pure and yet vigorous and graphic prose? The distance between this and Sir Walter Raleigh is not so great; the distance between the best and the worst in our day is immeasurable.

And yet the good is still good; and there are even religious writers who at least know where to go for their models. Some of the writings of the late Bishop Hensley Henson are still worth reading for their purity and vigour of diction. And here is a more recent example, from a sermon by Dr Austin Farrer:

The other night we were sitting in the theatre watching the ballet, and almost equally amazed at two things: the beautiful rhythmic freedom of the dancers, and the stolidity of the audience. Perhaps their hearts were dancing within then, but if so, you couldn't see it on their faces. As for the performers, goodness, what a pleasure it must be to reach such a pitch of art, and trust your limbs to float and twinkle through the lovely maze of movement. What a release, and yet at the same time what a control! . . .

Try listening to silence. It is supposed to be silent in my house when I sit thinking of my sermon; but the silence is all rhythm, one rhythm overlaying another. The clock ticks on the shelf, a car faintly audible from a great distance purrs its way down under my window and off again into space and darkness. The poor tin clarinet of a little old man up the street is quavering a

hymn-tune. There is a background of pattering rain. There is
the beating of my heart. I can capture and isolate one rhythm
after another by selective attention. Prayer is something like
that—listening to silence.[15]

It is in the context of all these different kinds and levels of contemporary style that the translators of the *NEB* have had to work. And
to judge how successful they have been is really to judge which of
these different styles the translation comes nearest to reproducing.

On one thing most commentators have been agreed: the
language of the *NEB* may be contemporary speech but it has lost
the resonance of 'declaimed' speech, and is in many places thin and
echo-less for reading aloud, especially in a church or during a
service. It is not altogether fair to put passages of the AV and the
NEB and compare them, since the *NEB* does not pretend to be a
revision of AV (or of any other version) but a fresh translation. Yet
it is difficult otherwise to make the loss clear. Here, for instance, is
the new version of Colossians 3^{1-4}:

> Were you not raised to life with Christ? Then aspire to the
> realm above, where Christ is, seated at the right hand of God,
> and let your thoughts dwell on that higher realm, not on this
> earthly life. I repeat, you died; and now your life lies hidden with
> Christ in God. When Christ, who is our life, is manifested, then
> you too will be manifested with him in glory.

This is not one of the worst passages. But that is partly because it in
fact (intentionally or not) sticks fairly closely to the rhythms, even
the language of the old version. But where it does not it falls flat:
'aspire', 'higher realms'—abstract words. And the tiresome,
prosaic, 'I repeat'. Indeed the retention of a segment of AV in the
middle of this has the effect of what Mr Steiner calls 'burning a
hole in their own drab page'.[16]

Another well-known passage is a good test-case. Here is
Romans 8^{31-5}. AV first:

> What shall we then say to these things? If God be for us, who
> can be against us? . . . Who shall lay anything to the charge of

---

[15] A. M. Farrer, *Said or Sung*, (1960), pp. 185–7.
[16] G. Steiner, *The Death of Tragedy*, p. 314.

God's elect? It is God that justifieth. Who is he that condemneth? It is Christ that died, yea, rather, that is risen again, who is even at the right hand of God, who also maketh intercession for us. . . .

For I am persuaded, that neither death, nor life, nor angels, nor principalities, nor powers, nor things present, nor things to come, nor height, nor depth, nor any other creature, shall be able to separate us from the love of God, which is in Christ Jesus our Lord.

Now the *NEB*:

With all this in mind, what are we to say? If God is on our side, who is against us? . . . Who will be the accuser of God's chosen ones? It is God who pronounces acquittal: then who can condemn? It is Christ—Christ who died, and, more than that, was raised from the dead—who is at God's right hand, and indeed pleads our cause. . . .

For I am convinced that there is nothing in death or life, in the realm of spirits or superhuman powers, in the world as it is or the world as it shall be, in the forces of the universe, in heights or depths—nothing in all creation that can separate us from the love of God in Christ Jesus our Lord.

This seems to me flat, at least to begin with. The opening phrase, for instance, 'With all this in mind, what are we to say?' It sounds like a Chairman summing up after a long discussion. And listen to the jagged rhythm of 'It is God who pronounces acquittal: then who can condemn'. It sounds like wagons jostling one another in a goods yard.

Here is another hideously unrhythmical passage, from 2 Corinthians 6[8]: 'Honour and dishonour, praise and blame, are alike our lot.' In 2 Corinthians 8[15], we cannot help making a comparison in our minds with the old version:

The man who got much had no more than enough, and the man who got little did not go short.

He that had gathered much had nothing over, and he that had gathered little had no lack.

It isn't only the rhythm that is clumsy: the whole thing is so wordy, twenty words to say what the AV said in seventeen.

Sometimes the loss in linguistic vigour is also a loss in authority. Consider the passage that has so often comforted mourners:

> But I would not have you to be ignorant, brethren, concerning them which are asleep, that ye sorrow not, even as others which have no hope (1 Thess 4¹³).

In the *NEB* this is:

> We want you not to remain in ignorance, brothers, about those who sleep in death; you should not grieve like the rest of men, who have no hope. . . .

Almost everything has been lost: not only the rhythm, but the sense of authority that goes with it—that bracing sense that we aren't appealing to ideas or vague hopes of our own but to firm promises and facts. It has become weak, feminine—like saying, 'Cheer up, children, it's not so bad after all'. There is another phrase in 2 Corinthians (7²) which suffers from a similar weakness: the AV has 'Receive us'. *NEB* has 'Do make a place for us in your hearts'—both long-winded, abstract, and lacking in that sense of apostolic command.

Doubters, too, need the challenge of divine authority, not vague exhortation. When a man brings his epileptic son to be cured,

> Jesus said unto him, If thou canst believe, all things are possible to him that believeth. And straightway the father of the child cried out, and said with tears, Lord, I believe; help thou mine unbelief (Mk 9²³⁻⁴).

In the new version this becomes:

> 'If it is possible!' said Jesus. 'Everything is possible to one who has faith.'
> 'I have faith,' cried the boy's father; 'help me where faith falls short.'

This is meant to be conversational language: but would anyone in fact talk like that today? And the pungency of the original—'I believe—help my unbelief'—has been lost, without any gain in twentieth-century immediacy. There is a similar loss in the case of 'doubting Thomas'. When Thomas is sceptical whether the figure appearing to the disciples is really the risen Lord, Jesus says: 'Reach hither thy hand, and thrust it into my side: and be not faithless, but believing' (Jn. 20²⁷). In the *NEB* this becomes: '. . . reach your hand here and put it into my side; be unbelieving no longer, but believe.'

There are many places where the new translation is a periphrasis or even a comment, rather than a translation: and whenever this happens there is a stylistic loss as well. 'Christ in you, the hope of glory' (Col 1²⁷) becomes 'Christ in you, the hope of a glory to come.' (There is no 'to come' in the Greek: and the plain translation is more challenging). In Ephesians 6¹¹, for 'put on the whole armour of God', the *NEB* has 'put on all the armour which God provides'. This is, no doubt, a gloss on the particular form of the Greek genitive used, but it seems to me pedantic and I suspect that it may even be a narrowing down of St Paul's imagery. When, again, St Paul is arguing for the resurrection he says that 'If Christ be not raised, your faith is vain; ye are yet in your sins.' The *NEB* has him say: 'If Christ was not raised, your faith has nothing in it and you are still in your old state of sin'. Surely to 'be in sin' conveys something much more graphic, and more disastrous, than merely 'to be in a state of sin': and it is the former that the Greek conveys. In Romans 12¹⁰ St Paul speaks of Christian relationships, and urges the faithful: 'Be kindly affectioned one to another with brotherly love; in honour preferring one another.' The *NEB* has a much more prosy exhortation: 'Let love for our brotherhood breed warmth of mutual affection. Give pride of place to one another in esteem.'

Sometimes the attempt to be up to date and colloquial is no less disastrous. In the discussion between two disciples, walking to Emmaus, and the stranger who joins them, the latter (who of course is really Jesus) asks them what they have been talking about and why they look so sad.

One, called Cleopas, answered: 'Are you the only person staying in Jerusalem not to know what has happened there in the last few days?' 'What do you mean?' he said. 'All this about Jesus of Nazareth,' they replied (Luke 24¹⁸⁻¹⁹).

And after describing the women's report that they had found the tomb empty, they ended

'So some of our people went to the tomb and found things just as the women had said' (24²⁴).

'All this about', 'found things'—the flabby, slang expressions are no doubt meant to reproduce the down-to-earth Aramaic of the original: but I don't think it comes off. Nor does the expression put in our Lord's lips at Matthew 9²⁴; 'And when Jesus came into the ruler's house, and saw the minstrels and the people making a noise, He said unto them, Give place: for the maid is not dead, but sleepeth. . . .' The *NEB* has: 'When Jesus arrived at the president's house and saw the flute-players and the general commotion, he said, "Be off! The girl is not dead: she is asleep."' 'Be off!'—It sounds like my cat-loving maiden aunt shooing dogs away from the garden.

The criticism that has most constantly been directed at the *NEB* has been its employment of what has been called the 'language of administrators'. Here are a few of the examples: 'And there are many other points on which they have a traditional rule to maintain' (Mk 7⁴); 'They brought to him a man who was deaf . . . *with the request that* he would lay his hand . . .' (Mk 7³²); Herod 'ascertained' the time from the astrologers (Mt 2⁷,¹⁶), and told them to 'report to him' (Mt 2⁸). One of the worst examples is in 1 Corinthians 14¹⁷: St Paul has been discussing the unintelligible glossolalia, and asking what is the use of public prayers which no one can understand. The AV has 'For thou verily givest thanks well, but the other is not edified.' The *NEB*: 'Your prayer of thanksgiving may be all that could be desired, but it is no help to the other man.' 'All that could be desired'—it sounds like a schoolmaster's end-of-term report on a pupil's behaviour. In Acts 15, where in fact the Church has to have a sort of Committee meeting to decide about conditions for letting Gentiles become Christians, it is perhaps fair to expect 'committee-ese': 'The apostles and elders held a meeting to look into this matter; and, after a long debate . . . etc.' (Acts 15⁶); but one almost expects: 'After the Minutes of the previous Meeting were read and approved.' And at any rate this sort of language is not justified in other contexts: 'This Judas, *be it noted*, after buying a plot of land . . .' (Acts 1¹⁸); 'So the Twelve called the whole body of disciples together and said, "It would *be a grave mistake* for us to neglect the word of God . . .".' (Acts 6²); 'On the second visit Joseph was recognized by his brothers, and *his family connections were disclosed* to Pharaoh' (Acts 7¹³); '"You and your money", said Peter sternly to Simon Magus, who wanted to buy the Holy Spirit's power: "You and your money . . . *may you come to a bad end*, for thinking God's gift is for sale!"' (Acts 8²⁰). It would be interesting, too, to add up the number of times that a concrete word or phrase in the Greek is altered to an abstract word in the English. A good example is καλῶν ἔργων (Heb 10²⁴), which becomes 'active goodness'—and incidentally thereby dodges an important, if painful, theological controversy which had a good deal to do with the Reformation!

It was perhaps to be expected that the poetry would fare worst—though it augurs ill for the fate of the Old Testament under the hands of the same translation committee. The quasi-poetic language of the Prologue to St John's Gospel is a good example—and what the *NEB* makes of that is well known. Curiously enough, the most difficult poetic passage, the *Magnificat*, is on the whole the least unsuccessful—the translation is not particularly felicitous but it is not positively jarring. But what about:

This day, Master, thou givest thy servant his discharge in peace; now thy promise is fulfilled.
For I have seen with my own eyes the deliverance which thou hast made ready in full view of all the nations:
A light that will be a revelation to the heathen, and glory to thy people Israel (Lk 2²⁹⁻³²)

And worse still, the song of the heavenly host:

Glory to God in highest heaven,
And on earth his peace for men on whom his favour rests (Lk 2¹⁴).

The only comfort is that we shall never be expected to sing these to Anglican chants or plainsong.

Is there nothing that we can put on the credit side of the balance sheet? There is much. If there is loss of poetry, as there almost always is, there is often a gain not only in clarity but in bluntness.

Some non-Christian critics have bewailed the disappearance of the old language—partly, one suspects, because it was vague, distant, and 'symbolic' enough not to challenge them about its truth. One such writer, speaking of the Authorized Version, said: 'In its remoteness . . . incantations, music, involutions and obscurities were its spell as well as its drudgery.'[17] Perhaps the advantage of the *NEB* will be that, in its starkness, nudity, it won't let people get away with 'merely symbolic' adherence to what the Bible says.

When they heard this they were cut to the heart, and said to Peter and the Apostles, 'Friends, what are we to do?' 'Repent', said Peter, 'repent and be baptized, every one of you' (Acts 2[37]).

There's no getting round that. It seems to me significant, too, that one of the most effective passages in the *NEB* is a piece of straightforward narrative, of good story-telling—the account of the shipwreck in Acts 27.

Are these positive virtues, however, enough to save the translation from its literary critics? This is a question each must answer for himself; my own answer is, reluctantly, No. And for this reason: that I believe the Christian Church has a profound responsibility towards a people's language, and I cannot see an awareness of this responsibility in this translation. 'Any radical change in poetic form', says T. S. Eliot, 'is likely to be the symptom of some very much deeper change in society and in the individual.'[18] What is true of poetic form is true also of prose style. It is as serious a matter to corrupt a people's language as it is to corrupt a people's behaviour. Perhaps more serious: because it is fairly easy to register when a generation is becoming anti-social, when 'fiddling' becomes respectable, or general moral standards are declining; but when words begin to decay or rhythms begin to go loose and soggy, no one notices and the poison spreads. If the Word of God truly speaks through the Bible, then He will speak a word of challenge to men's minds as well as to their hearts and wills: and how men's minds work is revealed in what their words say. Far from canonizing, or exploiting, the flaccid, vague language of our time, the Bible should be constantly showing it up, directing an arc-light upon it, cauterizing its impurities. It can be said that our Lord's

[17] V. S. Pritchett, in *The New Statesman*, 17th March 1961.
[18] *The Use of Poetry and the Use of Criticism* (1933), p. 75.

answers to the scribes and Pharisees frequently take the form of either literary criticism or linguistic analysis. 'Is it lawful to pay tribute?' *Reply*: 'What do you mean by *lawful*?' 'In the resurrection whose wife shall she be?' *Reply*: 'What do you mean by *wife*?' He is judging their language as it reflects their muddled, or dishonest concepts. To produce a new translation which shall only speak to the remnant, to the gathered Church, to the select few is ultimately to evade a responsibility to the whole of society: and part of that responsibility is to its manner of speech. And in the end it is the Bible itself which will teach us how the Bible is to be rendered. For (and here, as if taking inspiration from the very meaning of the passage, the rendering of the *NEB* is admirable),

The word of God is alive and active. It cuts more keenly than any two-edged sword, piercing as far as the place where life and spirit, joints and marrow, divide. It sifts the purpose and thoughts of the heart. There is nothing in creation that can hide from him; everything lies naked and exposed to the eyes of the One with whom we have to reckon (Heb 4[12ff]).

Saturday Review[1]

F. L. LUCAS

...**R**ELIGIOUS OR doctrinal aspects are beyond my competence; I can only discuss the book as a job of translation.

NEB: '*Consider how the lilies grow in the fields* . . . and yet, I tell you, even Solomon in all his *splendour* was not *attired* like one of these.' *KJB:* '*Consider the lilies of the field*, how they grow . . . And yet I say unto you, That even Solomon in all his *glory* was not *arrayed* like one of these.' (*RSV* is here almost identical with *KJB*.)

NEB: '*Do not feed your pearls to pigs*: they *will only* trample on them, and turn and *tear you to pieces*.' *KJB:* '*Neither cast ye your pearls* before *swine*, *lest* they trample them under their feet, and turn again and *rend you*.' *RSV:* '*Do not throw* your pearls before *swine*, *lest* they trample them underfoot and turn to *attack you*.'

It at once becomes clear that the new Bible departs much farther from King James's than did the *Revised Standard*. It also departs farther from the literal Greek. Going farther, in my opinion, it fares worse; and gains nothing whatever. 'Consider the lilies, how . . .' is (1) nearer the Greek; (2) more vivid; (3) more parallel with 'Look at the birds'. Why 'grow in the fields'? Where else would they grow? In pots? The Greek says, 'lilies of the field'. Why change 'his glory' to 'his splendour'? It is no more accurate; and 'his splendour' hisses, with its double 's'. Why 'feed' pearls, when the Greek says 'cast' or 'throw'? Why change 'swine' to 'pigs'? 'They *will only* trample' is a mistranslation. *KJB* and *RSV* were right. The Greek means '*for fear they should* trample'. It is a risk; not a certainty. Pigs too have caprices. They might just run away. Why change 'rend' to 'tear to pieces', when 'rend' is right, and the other is not? One could multiply for hours such instances of apparently wanton alteration, often for the worse. One hesitates to criticize the work of a whole bevy of bishops, a whole posse of professors. But I am dismayed.

[1] 1st April 1961, pp. 12–14.

Try again. *NEB:* 'You are salt *to the world.* . . . You are light *for all the world.*' *RSV:* 'You are *the* salt *of the earth.* . . . You are the light of the world.' This last is absolutely literal. The Greek says 'of', not 'to' or 'for'. 'Salt of the earth' has become part of the English language. Why say 'world' twice over, when the Greek is at pains to avoid this 'vain repetition' by using 'earth' in the first phrase, 'world' in the second? Why say '*all* the world' when the Greek says simply 'the world'? These tamperings add no accuracy, no clarity, no beauty—much the reverse. They seem to me what Johnson called 'the fury of innovation'. *NEB:* 'Anyone who *nurses anger* against his brother *must be* brought to judgement.' *RSV:* 'Every one who is *angry* with his brother *shall be liable* to judgement.' 'Must' seems to me wrong—it sounds like a police chief briefing his constables. The Greek says, like *RSV*, 'be liable to'.

Again, in *NEB* the Prodigal Son begins 'to feel the pinch', where *RSV* quite simply, and rightly, renders 'to be in want'. Why try to enliven the passage with this dull, dead metaphor? There is not even its ghost in the Greek. In *NEB* the Prodigal's brother talks of his running through money 'with his women'. The Greek says bluntly 'harlots'. The difference is surely obvious. 'His women' need not imply harlots; and harlots might have ill deserved to be called '*his*' women'. Obviously I am a pedant. But I believe that translators should be careful about nuances, and not blur shades of meaning.

Turn to Dives and Lazarus. The new version says Lazarus '*would have been* glad' to eat the rich man's scraps; implying that he was not allowed to. The Greek states only that he wanted to eat them; there is nothing to suggest that he was prevented. Why libel poor Dives, on no evidence? The new version makes Abraham say to Dives in Hell that in life he had '*all* the good things', and Lazarus '*all* the bad'. 'What!' one wonders; 'was *no* blessing whatsoever missed by Dives, *no* misery in the world spared to Lazarus?' Look at the Greek, or *KJB* or *RSV*. Neither of these absurd 'all's' is there. The Greek says: '. . . in life you had *your* good things; Lazarus, the bad.' Which makes sense.

Like an inverted Balaam, I came hoping to bless, and have so far been compelled to curse. It is a relief, therefore, to reach the difficult first five verses of St John and find a rendering (too long to quote) that, though rather audaciously free, seems unusually readable and clear. But, as one searches on, the fog re-descends;

though not quite so dismally as in the Gospels. St Paul tells the Athenians: '. . . in everything *that concerns religion* you are uncommonly scrupulous.' 'That concerns religion' is slipped in here by the translators. But the real meaning seems: '*In all matters* you are particularly in awe of the divine.' (For instance, Athens once lost a whole army through superstition about lunar eclipses.) To the Corinthians St Paul wrote the famous phrase: 'Death is swallowed up in victory.' So the Greek. But this now becomes: 'Death is swallowed up; victory is won!' Why? St Paul wrote: 'But *some man will say*, "How are the dead raised?" . . . *Fool! . . .*' (In the Greek, one word likewise—'ἄφρων!') Yet this now becomes: 'But, *you may ask*, how are the dead raised? . . . A *senseless question!*' No doubt, politer. But how curious thus to emend, and emasculate, the Apostle's manners!

These are only a handful of the possible examples. I have tried to deal with facts rather than style, truth rather than beauty. For about truth one can argue; about beauty one cannot. But, for style, here is one instance: 'Come unto me, all ye that labour and are heavy laden, and I will give you rest.' A faithful, faultless rendering of the Greek. This is now improved to 'Come to me, all whose work is hard, whose load is heavy; and I will give you *relief*.' It ruins that beauty of rhythm which has helped the memories of generations, and kept the Bible running in their heads. And why 'relief'? It is not one tittle more correct—in my view, less correct. (Elsewhere the translators render this same Greek word themselves as 'rest'.) 'Relief'! A term associated with things like 'outdoor relief', and the 'instant relief' promised by patent medicines. In prosaic prose, a useful drudge of a word; but here?

Conceivably, of course, *some* of these alterations (such as 'you are salt to the world') *might* be based on textual changes in the Greek; which *might* be right. But, if so, why not give a few explanatory examples in the introduction? As it is, one suspects, rather, the same sort of insensitiveness as made Dr Moffatt alter Job's 'Why died I not from the womb?' into 'Why was I not buried like an abortion?' . . .

The *New English Bible* avoids the worst of such modernizing excesses, but not all. Often it seems to me to alter wantonly, and for the worse—to exchange dignity, or beauty, for a banal breeziness—to stagger into wordiness, imprecision or downright untruth. At moments it made me remember that great man William Morris

striding through some 'restored' English church and growling
'Beasts! Pigs! Damn their souls!' That, however, would be unfair
to the sincere men who have toiled thirteen years on this work, and
to the admirable designing of the book by the University Presses
of my mother Cambridge and my aunt Oxford. It is unfortunate
to have had to say what I have. But it would, I feel, be far more
unfortunate if this version came into general, public use.

Church Times[1]

J. B. PHILLIPS

...IN ASSESSING this work we need to remember that it
represents the result of thirteen years' labour of the best
scholars and the finest masters of English style which the British
Isles can afford. This is no effort made by an individual with a
passion for communication, but the studied and deliberate production of a team of experts. For this reason we approach it with
both critical and appreciative faculties set to maximum sensitivity.
We have a right to expect the best.

The Introduction to the New Translation can be profitably
compared with the Dedication to the version of King James's men.
Not only have our modern scholars access to more and better
manuscripts than were available 350 years ago, but their whole
attitude towards translating the Word of God is quite different. The
men of 1611, confronted with the living oracles of God, did their
utmost to turn the Greek into the most beautiful, euphonious and
majestic English that they knew. Their attitude is comparable with
that of the pre-Reformation monk who would spend a lifetime
writing his Latin manuscript with incredible pains and decorate it
with dedicated artistry.

Our modern translators, quite rightly in my opinion, have pur-
sued with no less reverence a different course. I am glad to notice,
from the modest and somewhat disarming Introduction, that the idea
of 'timeless English' has been dropped. Of course there is no such
thing. The translators indeed admit that 'the rate of change in English usage has accelerated'. Today's translators have been concerned
to turn what was contemporary Greek into what is contemporary
English, and in this they have for the most part succeeded admirably.

They have avoided the consistent but unrealistic beauty of style
which pervades the whole of the Authorized Version. They have,
for example, preserved the strength and terseness of Mark. They
have hinted at the comparative prolixity of Matthew, and they
have fairly reproduced the verbal artistry of Luke. And in the

[1] 17th March 1961, pp. 13–16.

Gospel of John the change of style from an economical narrative into a more polished discursive manner is at once apparent. Throughout the Epistles the note of urgency and the sense of concern for the young Church is well conveyed. And in the Book of Revelation there is no dilution of the high poetry and awe-inspiring beauty of heavenly things.

The paragraphing of the new version is really excellent, and the page headings, while not in the least obtrusive, are very useful. For example, there are *The Gospel according to Paul* (*Romans*), *Recall to Fundamentals* (*1 John*), *Practical Religion* (*James*), *Growing Tension* (*Mark* 7), and very many more.

It is also good to see Old Testament quotations rendered into modern English. This not only makes them far more intelligible, but whets the appetite for the new version of the Old Testament which we understand is at this moment in preparation.

Because of the important position the new translation is bound to command, it is one's duty to draw attention to what appear to be minor faults. Homer may nod, and be quickly forgiven. But, where there is a *posse* of Homers, especially commissioned to keep one another on the alert, there should be no failure in style or in accuracy. The faults I have to find are irritating blemishes on an otherwise splendid piece of work. Obviously within the space of a short article I can only include a few criticisms. . . .

If I have been critical, I hope I have also been appreciative. After reading and re-reading this translation I am left in no doubt but that it is a magnificent and memorable accomplishment. There is an evenness of texture which runs through the whole volume—not, of course, the evenness of style which is so evident in the version of 1611, but a kind of common spiritual authority which binds the various authors together. They obviously have access to the same living God. If they speak in different ways they speak with one voice, and that voice speaks unerringly to the innermost heart of man.

All in all I see no loss of spiritual potency in this rendering of the New Testament into the English of today; indeed I see great gain. Striking and priceless truths, which have lain dormant for years in the deep-freeze of traditional beauty, spring to life with fresh challenge and quite alarming relevance to the men of the jet age. There is no need to argue about inspiration, for the Word of God is out of its jewelled scabbard and is as sharp, as powerful and as discerning as ever.

Studia Evangelica[1]

C. L. WRENN

...WHILE SHARING the feeling of admiration for this work of selfless scholarship and piety which has been so widely expressed, I propose in what follows to examine briefly some aspects both in the theory and the practice of the translators which I think of real importance, which have not yet received the attention they call for.

First, I would ask: is it really desirable and feasible to employ 'the natural vocabulary, constructions and rhythms' of the speech of today to render the basic documents of our faith ? The late Monsignor Ronald Knox saw some part of the difficulty when he sought for a 'timeless' language for his own translation, while preserving with minimal change the language of specially sacred passages which familiar tradition has hallowed. He looked for language which might seem intelligible to both the seventeenth century and to us today. So much of our natural speech is flat, trivial and unstable: and the spoken language changes so much more quickly than the written. It has often been noticed of late that the language of the New Testament with its metaphors and similes expresses a thought-pattern which is not receivable by 'the common man' of today without great effort. There has been a spiritual contraction in the recent centuries which has made the whole mental climate of the New Testament alien; so that the appropriate elements for its expression in the 'natural vocabulary' of speech scarcely exist. With the loss of awareness of the supra-phenomenal world, for the expression of which allegory and symbolism had been found necessary, the effective linguistic tools have become unusable or defunct. If passages of the Scriptures are to suggest things of supra-phenomenal reality, it cannot well be done in the natural vocabulary of our current speech. It must, perforce, employ a language no longer current. A purely synchronic language is, in fact, not feasible with our changing fashions of speech.

[1] Vol. III (1964), pp. 288–95.

Here is a simple illustration of what I am trying to convey, from St Mark 8[36]. The *NEB* reads: 'What does a man gain by winning the whole world at the cost of his *true self*.' The AV (based on slightly different Greek) has: 'For what shall it profit a man if he shall gain the whole world, and lose *his own soul*.' Our current habit of speech does not easily treat of the soul: so the Greek ψυχή is here rendered 'true self'. I am not forgetting that some recent researches have seemed to point to this rendering on the assumption that the Greek concept was influenced by Aramaic in which the corresponding word would have meant something like 'personality' or 'true self'. But *anima* and the terms for 'soul' in modern languages had been the view of the Church for some 1,800 years. Thus it is that a basic Christian concept may seem to have been blurred or weakened for the sake of contemporaneity.

Related to this kind of 'up-to-dateness' is, as I think, the error of assuming that certain fundamental Greek words, with their Latin Patristic equivalents, had remained static in meaning since pre-Christian times. Such words are ἀγάπη (*caritas*, charity) χάρις (*gratia*, grace) and πειρασμός (*tentatio*, temptation) which are supposed to retain their 'original' senses of 'love', 'favour' and 'test' or 'ordeal'. But already in the Apostolic age χάρις had begun to assume some of the connotations of divine Grace, as seems to be admitted universally in rendering the closing words of 2 Corinthians, and as 'Grace' it remained till the Reformation.[2] Indeed, Tyndale, usually a strong stickler for literalness in handling '*Graeca veritas*', yet makes Gabriel salute Our Lady in the Lucan account of the Annunciation as 'full of grace' (Lk 1[28]) in rendering the Greek participle κεχαριτωμένη though the AV has 'highly favoured'. Incidentally, the rendering in the *NEB*, 'Greetings, most favoured one', may be thought to be a long way from 'the natural vocabulary, constructions and rhythms of contemporary speech'. Similarly, the ἀγάπη of 1 Corinthians 13 very early was taken as *Caritas*, 'Charity', the 'theological virtue'. This time it was Tyndale who led the way in rendering it as 'love', while the AV followed Rheims in restoring 'Charity'. With the Greek πειρασμός the situation is somewhat different; for though the Latin verb *tentare* was in good classical use, its abstract noun *tentatio* was an almost entirely Christian development, expressing both 'testing'

---

[2] At the end of 2 Corinthians Tyndale replaced 'favour' of his 1525 edition with 'grace' in the 1534 revision.

and 'tempting'. When 'temptation', especially in the *Pater Noster*, has had such wide connotations throughout Christian history, one may doubt the wisdom of replacing it contextually by the narrower and (supposedly) more exact rendering. The *NEB* in the Lord's Prayer has 'Do not bring us to the *test*', in both the longer St Matthew version and the shorter one of St Luke; yet Jesus is 'tempted' by Satan in Mark 1[13] where the Greek has the participle, πειραζόμενος; and again in Luke 4[2]. In the Apocalypse, however, the same word πειρασμός is rendered 'ordeal' in 3[10]: 'I will keep you from the ordeal that is to fall upon the whole world.' Here the traditional translation of the Greek ἐκ τῆς ὥρας τοῦ πειρασμοῦ is 'from the hour of temptation'.

Secondly, I would wish for a kind of language that might retain if possible those sacramental and numinous elements needed naturally for the expression of sacred and mysterious religious truths. Tyndale, we are told, boasted to the priest of Gloucester that because of the effects of his vernacular translation 'A boy that driveth the plough shall know more of the Scriptures than thou dost'. Yet in all languages I know of it has been the universal tendency to express the central ideas of religion in a language more dignified, more archaic even, and with more implicit levels of meaning than that used for the doings of ordinary life. Many of Tyndale's colloquialisms were replaced in the AV by forms of more dignity and depth which were yet, even in the early seventeenth century, obsolescent or merely literary.

This is too well known to need illustration, I think. In the Middle Ages the opening verses of St John's Gospel were often unconsciously regarded as a kind of incantation for popular purposes: Chaucer's Friar, for instance, would bless a house he visited with his *In Principio:* and the special place of this prologue at the close of the Mass attests the feeling of its peculiar and fundamental sacredness which has been almost universal through-out Christian history. Here, therefore, is a case where particular care should be taken not to disturb the traditional rendering without very strong reason. I would not reject the incantatory aspects of this language, which persists through the Latin and our vernacular rendering till this century. The emotive language which stirs a consciousness of unsearchable sacredness and mystery is not necessarily inconsistent with truth, since there must be aspects of divine truth which are beyond expression in purely rational terms.

The rendering *Word*, for instance, for λόγος has been universal in English since early Anglo-Saxon times: and the *NEB* rightly preserves it; but otherwise it has lost the kind of emotive element I am concerned with. It begins: 'When all things began, the Word already was. The Word dwelt with God, and what God was, the Word was.' Now this is neat and skilful, yet not quite the style of natural current speech, nor does it retain the sacramental or numinous feeling proper for the conveying of the divine mystery. The fact is that this passage cannot effectively be 'modernized'. The depth and difficulty of its thought and feeling require a language in translation which is traditional and literary. Other recent attempts on it have been no more successful. The extremes of the weakness inherent in modernizing this passage are to be seen in the versions of Moffatt and of J. B. Phillips. Moffatt renders thus: 'The Logos existed in the very beginning. The Logos was with God. The Logos was divine.' Phillips has: 'At the beginning God expressed himself. That personal expression, that word, was with God, and was God, and he existed with God from the beginning.' This last effort, I think, well emphasizes the vast changes in thought-pattern which recent times have brought. In verse 5, to take a related type of difficulty, the usual English rendering till our century had been much as in the AV: 'And the light shineth in darkness, and the darkness *comprehended* it not', where 'comprehended', following the Vulgate of St Jerome, preserves the mystery of the Greek word κατέλαβεν. For in the clause ἡ σκοτία αὐτὸ οὐ κατέλαβεν it would seem that it might in this Hellenistic period mean either 'understood', 'overcame', or even both. Now 'comprehended' as an English rendering, like the Latin, may imply either or both of these meanings. The *NEB* reads: 'The light shines on in the dark; and the darkness *has never quenched it.*' Incidentally, 'quenched' is no longer in the natural vocabulary of our current speech though it remains in good literary use.

Thirdly, I would point out the ill effects, as it appears to me, of the mixture of current speech with elements of a more literary, academic or even technical type. We find some intrusion into the somewhat flat and ordinary prose of the *NEB* of expressions arising from the effort to be technically accurate in matters of little importance; and at the same time, some of the colloquialisms are so contemporary as to seem at times almost vulgar. Here are a few examples of what I am thinking of: '*Ascertained* from them the time when the star had appeared' (Mt 2⁷) for banality. 'This is my Son, my Beloved, *on whom my favour rests*' (Mt 3¹⁷) stiff and not current. 'The people rounded on them' (Mt 20³¹) and 'Why are you trying to *catch me out*?' (Mt 22¹⁸) for extreme colloquiality.³ The translators have not been able to achieve their linguistic aims with any consistency.

But the clearest example of academic influence bringing disaster occurs in the parable of the wheat and the 'tares' in St Matthew 13. St Jerome was unable to discover the meaning of the Greek ζιζάνια, so merely transliterated it as *zizania* (pl.). It has never been clear exactly what weed was understood by the first hearers of the parable, though modern researches seem to point to darnel. The traditional word was *cockle* or *corn cockle* (Old English *coccul*) which appeared in the earlier Wycliffite Bible as cockle or darnel as alternatives. But the Purvey version replaced *cockle* by *tares*. From Tyndale, *tares* has through the AV retained its place as the widely accepted word, though the Rheims version and its revisions have preferred the older *cockle*. Now neither *cockle* nor *tares* can be correct, though one may doubt the wisdom of trying to locate the exact force of *zizania*, as that it was a noxious weed proper to cornfields is what really matters. But the medieval commentators commonly took *zizania* as *lolium:* and the nearest kind of lolium to the need of the context seems to be *lolium temulentum*, which has sometimes been called in English rustic dialects *darnel*. I confess that, when I first read this parable in the *NEB* I had to look up *darnel* in a dictionary: nor has it been in current speech in the received standard language for a century. Perhaps, then, darnel is technically the nearest we can get to the unknown *zizania*; but I sympathize with Moffatt, who just said 'weeds'; or with Ronald Knox who left the traditional Roman Catholic version for 'tares', because, I take it, it had become part of the English literary inheritance. For the same reason, I suppose, Knox has substituted 'trespasses' for the literal rendering 'debts' in the Matthew Lord's Prayer, thus following Tyndale and the Anglican Book of Common Prayer as against both the AV and Rheims. But because the Hebrew mind associated debt with *sin*, which is literally also the word used in the shorter Lucan version,⁴ the *NEB* employs colloquial language here: 'Forgive us the wrong we have done, as

---

³ Greek τί με πειράζετε is not specially colloquial.   ⁴ Lk 11⁴.

we have forgiven those who have wronged us.' This is where modern scholarship leads: but perhaps 'wrong' in current speech lacks the necessary force and depth of 'debt', or 'trespass'—and certainly of 'sin'.

Again, in the Lord's Prayer the usual rendering 'daily bread' is needlessly (in a work of this kind) supplemented by the alternative in a footnote 'bread for the morrow'. St Jerome here, as was often his practice when meeting an unsolved difficulty, invents a Latin word which at once indicates his uncertainty in rendering the apparent *hapax legomenon* ἐπιούσιον. Taking οὐσία as *substantia* and ἐπι as *super*, he coins his effort at literal rendering in *panem supersubstantialem*, which he explains in his commentary as *panem super omnes substantias*: thus suggesting the alternative possibilities of spiritual or temporal bread. The *NEB* is concerned only to add the notion of bread for the morrow because recent scholarship has revived this. But St Jerome, when he came to the Lucan version of the *Pater Noster* had decided, it would seem, that 'daily', *quotidianum*, was right for the same word ἐπιούσιον: and the Gothic translation from as early as the late fourth century agrees with what was probably the correct literal meaning 'continuing' or 'habitual' (sinteins). In fact, however, this ἐπιούσιον was probably not a *hapax legomenon*. Not only was an Egyptian papyrus found with it in a kind of shopping list (though this was later destroyed by fire) but I have lately been told by a learned native that it is still in use in the Thessaly dialect as 'daily bread' but as a noun without ἄρτος. The phrase commonly used by peasants is, I am told, ἐργάζομαι τὸν ἐπιούσιον 'I work for my daily bread'. This may support the view that the word was colloquial, and is so rare in written documents just because it was colloquial. In the same prayer 'thy name be hallowed' of the *NEB* is about as archaic as the AV, with only the slight difference of word-order.

A strange product of this mixed language in the *NEB* is the preference for 'splendour' for the traditional 'glory' in rendering δόξα. This results in Romans 8[30] in 'To those whom he justified he has also *given his splendour*', where the expected 'glorified' is replaced by 'given his splendour' for the Greek ἐδόξασεν. The 'stewards of the mysteries of God', οἰκονόμους μυστηρίων θεοῦ appear in 1 Corinthians 4[1] in reduced and weakened form as 'stewards of the *secrets* of God'. Nevertheless, I must pay tribute in touching upon the Epistles to what is, I believe, the outstanding achievement of the *NEB* in making so many dark places, especially of St Paul, intelligible and usable.

My last difficulty is concerned with the purpose for which the *NEB* New Testament may properly be recommended, and the degree of authority which it may be conceived to hold. I think it may well happen that it may enjoy such authority in popular esteem as the immense prestige of the scholars who have created it and the wide Church support it has already received, together with far-flung publicity, will attach to it; and this despite the fact that the 'provisional judgements' of the translators of the *NEB* in no sense make any claim to be authoritative. There is, I believe, a very real danger that these judgements may yet be so regarded. . . .

English Churchman[1]

TERENCE H. BROWN

... A FEW representative passages are briefly examined in the following paragraphs, which may be sufficient to demonstrate how disastrously the translators have failed to substantiate the claims advanced for their translation.

MORE DIFFICULT THAN THE AUTHORIZED VERSION

In many places the homely Anglo-Saxon words have been displaced by stilted latinisms, and simple expressions exchanged for more difficult ones. Typical examples are:

Invoke (call upon), Machinations (lying in wait), Anxious to ingratiate (willing to do the Jews pleasure), Divine retribution (wrath of God), Subordinate (put under), Beneficent work (grace), Divinely potent to demolish (mighty before God to the pulling down), Indefatigable in confuting (mightily convinced), Constant fortitude (all patience), Primacy (firstborn), Refractory (oppose themselves), Effulgence of his splendour (brightness of his glory), Arrogates (takes), Malign (speak evil), Mercenary (covetous), Contaminated with sensuality (spotted by the flesh), Inscribed (written).

Perhaps the most astonishing specimen is in Acts 17[18]: 'A propagandist for foreign deities' (a setter forth of strange gods). . . .

PEDANTIC

Many of the alterations in the new translation may titillate the palate of the pedant, while doing nothing to make the English rendering more clear than the AV.

The nice distinction between burglars, thieves, and robbers (Mt 24[43], etc.), while of interest to lexicographers, is rather remote from current English usage. 'Transjordan' for 'the other side of Jordan' seems quite unnecessary. Pasturage (pasture), Thereupon (then), Populace (people), represent no improvement upon the old version.

[1] No. 61 (17th March 1961), pp. 3–4.

Outstanding examples of pompous pedantry are to be found in 1 Timothy 1⁹, Parricides and matricides; 4³, Inculcating abstinence; 6³, Pompous ignoramus; James 3⁸, Intractable evil; Revelation 18⁹, Smoke of her conflagration. . . .

NOT CONTEMPORARY ENGLISH

In many passages the 'Literary Advisers' have sanctioned words and phrases which have no place in current English usage. Their use of 'Ministrant' in Hebrews 1¹⁴, where AV has 'ministering' is a representative case. Other strange expressions are in Luke 3¹⁵, On the tiptoe of expectation; 19⁴⁶, Robbers' cave (savouring of the *Arabian Nights*); John 8⁴¹, Base-born; 1 Corinithians 5⁹, loose livers; 1 Timothy 1¹, True-born; 1¹¹, Eternal felicity; Hebrews 3⁵, Servitor (servant); Revelation 18¹⁶, Bedizened (decked). This last quotation should be read side-by-side with the pathetic lament that 'the work of the Church is hindered by the archaic language of the AV'. 'Decked' or 'Bedizened'—which is archaic?

CRUDE COLLOQUIALISMS

Strangely intermingled with the abstruse and archaic language of the new version there are countless expressions so crudely colloquial, awkward, indiscreet, and inappropriate, that the reverent reader of the Scriptures will be shocked and appalled that they should be approved by a joint committee representing the major denominations and some of the Bible Societies.

'Let us toss for it', said the soldiers (Jn 19²⁴). 'I sponged on no one', said the Apostle (2 Cor 11⁹). 'They left me in the lurch' (2 Tim 4¹⁶). 'This is more than we can stomach', said the disciples (Jn 6⁶⁰). 'You are crazy', they said to Rhoda (Acts 12¹⁵). 'They got wind of it' (Acts 14⁶). 'Tell her to come and lend a hand', said Martha (Lk 10⁴⁰). 'This touched them on the raw' (Acts 7⁵⁴).

The Son of God, in Revelation 2²⁷, is said to use the words, 'smashing them to bits', and in Matthew 20¹², 'who have sweated all day in the blazing sun', and in Luke 15¹⁴, 'to feel the pinch' (to be in want). Deacons are to abstain from 'money-grubbing' (1 Tim 3⁸). . . .

UNSEEMLY

The Translators of the Authorized Version were wise and discreet in their choice of English words to convey the meaning of the original in passages relating to subjects not normally publicly discussed in mixed company. This becoming restraint was discarded by the translators of the new version. Expressions now introduced into the translation will make it unsuitable for use in Sunday-schools, Bible classes and young people's associations. The work of the Church is more likely to be hindered by the use of the new translation than the old.

Instances will be found in Matthew 1²⁵, 21¹⁶, ³¹, ³²; Luke 2⁶; Romans 1²⁶, ²⁷; 1 Corinthians 6¹⁰; Galatians 5¹²; James 2²⁵, and Revelation 2².

LITERARY LOSSES

The translators appear to have overlooked the fact that the AV has been in use long enough to fix many expressions permanently in the language of the people without regard to their scriptural context. 'Pearls before swine' has become proverbial and is not improved by alteration to 'Pearls to pigs'. 'Tombs covered with whitewash' will not displace 'whited sepulchres'. Paul's 'thorn in the flesh' now becomes 'a sharp pain in my body'. These changes are annoying, and pointless.

Other beautiful expressions which have enriched our language and are now to be discarded are 'His unspeakable gift' (2 Cor 9¹⁵); 'the Royal Law' (James 2⁸); and 'Inasmuch' (Mt 25⁴⁰). Many of the words used in the AV with reference to vital doctrines of the faith are also lost. The reader will no longer find the words 'elect', 'justify', 'impute', 'redemption', 'regeneration' or 'book of life', in the New Testament. These are replaced by other terms which weaken the force of the truth revealed. . . .

IMPORTANT DOCTRINAL CHANGES

(1) *Relating to the Son of God*

The Greek μονογενής (only-begotten) is now reduced to 'only' (Jn 1¹⁴, 3¹⁶, etc.). Some scholars have endeavoured to prove that the Greek word was being used during and before the first century to signify 'only', although its precise etymological signification is 'only-begotten'. A few evangelical scholars have also swallowed the bait, notwithstanding its strong flavour of heresy. The case for this important alteration is unscriptural, illogical, fallacious and untenable, and the diluted rendering calls into question the fundamental doctrine of the eternal generation and Sonship of our Lord.

(2) *His Miraculous Birth*

A footnote to Matthew 1[16] (Library Edition) states, 'one early witness has—Joseph, to whom Mary, a virgin was betrothed, was the father of . . .'. This note casts serious doubt upon the Virgin Birth of our Lord. It is culled from *one* early witness. No doubt many strange and erroneous readings could claim *one* early witness, but this appears to be the only instance where the translators have considered the error of one early witness to be worthy of a place in their margin. The element of doubt is increased by the omission of the word 'first-born' from Matthew 1[25].

(3) *His Unique Divine Sonship*

Articles. In the new version the treatment of the articles and personal pronouns weakens the force of many vital passages revealing or referring to the deity of the Lord Jesus Christ. Matthew 27[54], A son of God. The Greek has no indefinite article.[2] It is not necessary to supply one in English. If the translators objected to the definite article, they could preserve the force of the passage without any article, as in their own John 10[36], 'God's son', and 19[7], 'Son of God'. Their treatment of the article is by no means consistent. Luke 4[16], To synagogue (Greek 'to the synagogue'); John 3[5, 6], Water and spirit (AV the Spirit); but Hebrews 1[2], 'In the Son' (where the article is not found in the Greek).

Pronouns. The reverent 'Thou' and 'Thee' and related verb endings are retained in the new version only when addressed to God the Father. These forms are thus preserved throughout John 17 and wherever the Son addresses the Father, but the Father always addresses the Son as 'You'. If the respectful 'Thou' is retained as a mark of honour to the Father, dare we forget our Lord's words in John 5, 'That all men should honour the Son, even as they honour the Father'?

In the new version Jesus teaches His disciples to say to the Father, 'Thy name be hallowed', but the Father speaks to the Son saying of John, 'He will prepare your way before you', (Mt 11[10]).

---

[2] Readers unfamiliar with Greek may like to know that the Greek language has no indefinite article, so that the Greek for 'son of God' is indistinguishable from the Greek for 'a son of God'. (Ed.)

A distinction is thus introduced between the correct manner of address to the Father and the correct address to the Son. Saul of Tarsus, hearing a voice from heaven and not knowing whose voice, nevertheless carefully distinguishes between the honour due to the Father and the Son and says in Acts 26[15], 'Tell me, Lord, who you are'.

The translators are not consistent in their handling of this matter, as will be seen in Acts 13[33] and Hebrews 1[5]. They would not profess to know whether these two statements were made by Paul, but all must agree that both passages quote the second Psalm. In the former we read, 'You are my son'; in the latter, 'Thou art my Son'. There is even inconsistency in the use of the capital letters.

The sponsors of this version claim that the work of the Church is hindered by the archaic language of the Authorized Version, but the new translation introduces elements of dangerous confusion which were not to be found in the old. The reader is still required to master 'Thou' and 'Thee' and the old verb endings throughout John 17 and elsewhere. It is thus admitted that they remain a part of the language of religion wherever English is spoken. The alleged difficulty is certainly not removed in the new translation. *Punctuation.* In the AV, Romans 9[5] declares that Christ is God. The new version changes the punctuation,[3] so that we read two sentences, one saying that the Messiah was of human descent from David and the other an ascription of praise to God, 'May God . . . be blessed for ever'. This adaptation of the text, together with the adoption of the earlier Revisers' 1 Timothy 3[16] 'He who was manifested', for the AV 'God was manifest in the flesh', will make the version more readily acceptable to Jehovah's Witnesses and other unitarians.

Readers will be glad, however, to note that John 3[16], excluded from our Lord's discourse by the quotation marks in the *RSV*, has now come back to us as spoken by the Son. Lamentably, the word 'only-begotten' shrinks to 'only', as mentioned above.

[3] This statement cannot mean that the *NEB* changes the punctuation of the original Greek, since Greek manuscripts had no punctuation, the reader being left to infer from the sense where the pauses were meant to come. So what must be meant here is that the *NEB*—in common, be it said, with the great majority of modern scholars—takes a different view as to where the pause was meant to come in Romans 9[5] from that taken by the authors of the AV. This is scarcely an 'adaptation of the text'. See further p. 46. (Ed.)

RETREAT FROM REFORMED FAITH

Quite indefensibly the new version has in Mt 16[18]: 'You are Peter, the Rock; and on this rock I will build my church'. The parallel passage in John 1[42] becomes ' "You shall be called Cephas" (that is, Peter, the Rock)', but AV 'Cephas, which is by interpretation a stone' has support from Alford and *RSV* 'Cephas, which means Peter'. The new version affirms that Peter was the rock upon which the Church was built. The Scriptures affirm that Christ Himself is the rock foundation of the Church. The prevailing anxiety to be conciliatory to Rome is carried too far when it is allowed to corrupt the plain teaching of God's Word.[4]

Another concession to Rome will be found in Acts 13[2], where the significance of the change will be more evident to those who have knowledge of earlier controversies around this text. The new version sees the disciples keeping a fast and '*offering* worship to the Lord'. (AV 'ministered', *RSV* 'were worshipping'). Pereira's RC Portuguese has 'sacrificed' and the Bordeaux NT had 'offered the Sacrifice'. RC propagandists have used this text to prove that the Apostles celebrated Mass, and their contention hinges upon the word '*offered*'.

'General baptism', Luke 3[21]; 'Solomon's Cloister', Acts 3[11]; and 'Priestly service', Romans 15[16], will all doubtless be of interest to RCs and Anglo-Catholics.

DOGMATIC BIAS

It must not be assumed that all of the changes made have been dictated by manuscript evidence newly to hand, or by scholarly research into the precise meaning of Greek words or by the requirements of good literary form. Countless alterations betray the dogmatic bias of the translators against the reformed faith of our fathers.

The Atonement

1 John 2[2], 'Propitiation' is weakened to 'remedy for the defilement

---

[4] What the *NEB* has done in these passages is to make an addition in each case designed to bring out the fact that Cephas and Peter are the Aramaic and Greek words respectively for 'rock' and so the fact that in the first passage there is a pun and in the second a simple translation from Aramaic into Greek. In Matthew 16[18] the same point could have been made by printing: 'You are Peter [= the Rock] . . .' Whether this is 'indefensible' is for the reader to decide. In any case, what 'the Scriptures affirm' in Matthew 16[18] is a matter of interpretation, not translation. (Ed.)

of our sins'. The Greek word used by John was earlier used by the LXX with reference to the atonement, propitiation and reconciliation symbolized by the OT sacrifices. The sense of reconciliation and satisfaction is lost in the new version. 'Redemption through his blood, even the forgiveness of sins', in Colossians 1^{14} becomes the weaker 'release' and 'the blood' disappears.

Imputed Righteousness

Matthew 5^{20}, 'Except your righteousness exceed . . .' becomes 'unless you show yourselves far better men'. This no longer leads the reader to Christ 'who is made unto us wisdom and righteousness'; or reminds one of the blessedness of the man unto whom 'the Lord imputeth righteousness without works'; or of Paul's contempt for the righteousness of the law. The sinner merely has to show himself to be a better man than the Pharisee. The vital doctrine is also obscured by the consistent suppression of the word 'imputed'.

Effectual Calling. The Scriptures reveal the Son of God calling sinners to repentance. Repentance is revealed as the gift of God. The calling and the gift are associated with justification. In the new version He merely 'invites' sinners to repent (Mt 9^{13}).

Faith is declared to be 'the gift of God'. The new version speaks of faith being 'awakened', suggesting that all men have some kind of dormant faith which merely needs to be aroused to active life (Acts 3^{16} and Romans 10^{17}). The truth that all men are by nature 'dead in trespasses and sins' is thus obscured. To believe now becomes 'to yield allegiance', John 1^{12}, suggesting that the sinner makes a concession, while the Scriptures really affirm that he receives a gift.

For obvious dogmatic reasons, the word 'receive' is carefully suppressed in favour of 'accept' (Lk 18^{17}; Jn 10^{38}, 12^{48}, 14^{11}; Acts $2^{36, 41}$, 8^{14}, 11^1; 2 Cor 11^4; Jas 1^{21}). The new terminology portrays the sinner having his inherent faith awakened, accepting the evidence, quietly accepting the message, yielding allegiance to Christ, exerting himself to clinch God's choice and calling (2 Pet 1^{10}). letting himself be built into God's house (1 Pet 2^5), and exhorted not to miss his chance of entering into rest (Heb 4^1). The sinner is now assumed to be able to undertake a large share in the work of his salvation, and is apparently less in need of election, justification, redemption, imputed righteousness, regeneration, and the mercy seat. All of these are therefore quietly eliminated. The Book has not merely been retranslated. It has been largely rewritten. The reader may feel entitled to enquire whether 'scholarly qualities alone' are sufficient equipment for the solemn and responsible task of translating the Divine Revelation.

NO ACKNOWLEDGEMENT OF DIVINE INSPIRATION

The Translators' Preface of the Authorized Version of 1611 reverently acknowledges the Divine Inspiration and authority of the Holy Scriptures as the Word of God, a gift from heaven. One seeks in vain for any such testimony in the new version. The preface and the long statement issued by the sponsors at the time of publication are silent on this subject. It does not therefore occasion any surprise that 2 Timothy 3[16] has again been reduced to an assertion of partial rather than plenary inspiration. That 'scholarly judgement' upon which the 'untrained layman' is invited to rely sometimes betrays the characteristics of the chameleon. AV, 'All scripture is given by inspiration'; RV, 'Every scripture inspired of God'; Moffatt, 'All Scripture is given by inspiration'; *Twentieth Century NT*, 'Everything that is written under divine inspiration'; *RSV* (1952), 'All Scripture is inspired by God'; and now the new version comes back to the weaker statement. In 1952 the consensus of scholarly opinion in forty Protestant denominations in America confirmed the Authorized Version of this text. In 1961 the consensus of scholarly opinion in the major denominations of Great Britain supports the contrary view, notwithstanding the fact that the earlier rendering is undoubtedly correct. . . .

THE MANUSCRIPTS

Some changes have been made in the text on the ground that some of the more recently recovered MSS, being of earlier date than those available in 1604, probably represent the original documents more reliably. Some scholars tend to oversimplify this problem and give the impression that this part of the subject is closed. This is far from true. In the new version the translators have adopted most of the new readings favoured by the nineteenth-century revisers and they have added a few of their own. They claim to have brought their 'scholarly judgement' to bear upon the available evidence so as to produce in doubtful cases, with a high degree of probability, the most likely text. Such judgement is fallible and the degree of probability variable, and partly conditioned by the translator's Christian experience, faith, and dogmatic environment.

Every alteration on MS grounds is a debatable subject, and no one is obliged to assume that the new version is better than the old because it adds 'Isaiah' in Mark 1^2; omits 'My words' in Mark 8^{38}, changes seventy to seventy-two in Luke 10^1; puts 'Chosen one' for 'Son of God' in John 1^{34}; 'Son of Man' for 'Son of God' in John 9^{35}; moves John 7^{53}-8^{11} to the end of the Gospel in a place of distinguished doubt; and embellishes the conclusion of Mark's Gospel with a confusing array of misgivings and hesitations.

We have read this translation through completely, comparing several hundred passages with the latest critical edition of the Greek and with the Authorized Version and eight modern versions. Our conviction is that if any have been hindered in their approach to the truth by the alleged 'barriers of language', more are likely to be hindered in their apprehension of the truth by the numerous and serious deficiencies of the new version.

This translation will be a great embarrassment to those professedly evangelical societies and literature distribution organizations which have committed themselves in advance to accept and circulate a version so utterly alien to the faith of our fathers and unacceptable to those who still cherish some respect for the old paths.

Australian Lutheran[1]

H. P. HAMANN

THIS REVIEW does not pretend to be a critical review. It is a review meant to give the average layman of our Church some idea of the new translation as soon as possible after publication, and it is the result of first impressions gained after dipping into the translation here and there. . . .

As for the accuracy of the translation, although in great part it cannot be faulted, nevertheless we must voice considerable disappointment in those sentences or sections which are of particular concern for us Lutherans. Many of the passages central to our doctrine of justification by faith seem strangely weaker in the *NEB* translation, e.g. Romans 1[17], 3[21-31], 2 Corinthians 5[21]. The translation of 1 Corinthians 10[16] quite destroys the strong testimony this passage bears in Greek to the Real Presence. Two of the Beatitudes must be regarded as downright failures— Matthew 5[3], 'How blest are those who know that they are poor'; and 5[6], 'How blest are those who hunger and thirst to see right prevail; they shall be satisfied'. It is unfortunate that a theology alien to that which we Lutherans believe to be that of the New Testament has found its way into the *NEB*. It is, of course, not suggested that there has been any deliberate attempt to introduce a sectarian theology into the *NEB*, but the fact is that it is very difficult for any one and any body of men to avoid translating the New Testament in accord with the inmost convictions of years; and this danger has not been altogether avoided by those responsible for the *NEB*.

The criticism voiced in the previous paragraph makes it impossible to recommend the *NEB* for liturgical use or for use as a basis of instruction in our schools. The AV will have to continue to do this duty. But the *NEB* can still be of great value as a help in the study and understanding of a great deal of the New Testament alongside the proved and trusted older version. But pastors and teachers will have to be on their guard when dealing with passages like those mentioned. . . .

[1] Vol. XLIX, No. 8 (19th April 1961), p. 112.

Index of New Testament Texts

Index of Passages from the O.T. and the Apocrypha quoted in the N.T.

Discussion of Chapter and Section Headings in N.E.B.

Index of New Testament Manuscripts, Versions, Translators, etc.